The Trouble with Taffies

Welsh Hooligan Gangs

By
Jeff Marsh

www.hooligancentral.co.uk

Published in February 2009 by Head-Hunter Books
Copyright © 2009 Martin King and Jeff Marsh.
The moral right of the author has been asserted.

ISBN 978-1-906085-16-2

Head-Hunter Books
www.headhunterbooks.co.uk

Printed in Great Britain by
Athenaeum Press Limited

Jeff Marsh
bouncingbomb@hotmail.co.uk

Contents

According to Cambridge Advance Learner's Dictionary ...
Definition
Taffy
noun [C] (ALSO **Taff**) UK OFFENSIVE
a Welshman

According to Wikipedia ...
Taffy' (a merging of the common Welsh name
'Dafydd' and the Welsh river 'Taff') has since
become a derogatory term for a Welsh person.

Acknowledgments

I'd like to say thanks to everyone who has helped me put together this book even though I have never met some of you and have only spoken to you online or on the 'dog and bone'.

Thanks to Annis for putting me in touch with Martin King and making this book possible and also for the stories he's contributed. Thanks to Martin King for believing in me and publishing this book and John Barnes for his typesetting skills and hard graft.

Special thanks to Gaffa for his front page photo of the Old Bill attacking the boys.

Thanks to the Jacks who begrudgingly helped and to the ones I pinched photos from; special thanks to Stacko's son Liam. Thanks to all the Jacks for the fun time we've had kicking fuck out of you over the years and to Andrew Tooze for making me laugh with his book.

Thanks to the Newport lads who helped, to Korky, Farley and the DYC for all your stories and also Brian the Bluebird from Newport for his historical tales. Thanks to the Wrexham lads who have helped even though I never met you personally. It's appreciated.

Special thanks to all the Cardiff lot I've met over the years. There are far too many to mention all but I'll have a little go. The Ely Trendies, Seaside Section, Dibs, Morgan and the Bridgend Crew, Neath lads, The Maesteg Headers, The Fishing Crew, The PVM, Simmo and his lot, Deacon, Mac, Kenny, Luke, Alex and the youth, Chunky and the Ponty lads, Jinks for his horror ordeal in Jackland, Kersy for the stories and for being one of the original Swimmers (legendary status), Meic Gough, author of 'Patches Checks and Violence', The Merthyr lads, all the Valley Commandos, Trumpton riots and Bangor Warfare, Dessie, Quinny and the Dockers boys, Nils and the Dirty 30, Holyhead lads, The Legand, Stan and Pontypool/Cwmbran boys, The Penarth boys, all the non-football lads who've helped out in scraps over the years and everyone else.

If I've left anyone out, I'm sorry but you all know who you are.

Chapter One
Introduction

If you've read my first book "Soul Crew Seasiders", you'll know all about me. In case you haven't, allow me to introduce myself. My name is Jeff Marsh and for nearly 30 years I have been involved in one way or another with various hooligan gangs including Cardiff City's notorious Soul Crew.

A lot of people hate the Welsh, mainly because they don't understand us and a lot of hooligan firms have had the shock of their lives after travelling here. They have this vision of it being a few scruffy farmhouses on a hillside and a few sheep farmers to beat up. On arrival, they find massive mobs waiting for them because hooligans have travelled from far and wide in the hope of a scrap.

Welsh people are very territorial and have fought off invaders for thousands of years. I have looked at the historical roots of this hatred of the English, the holiday homes arson campaign of yesteryear and the Welsh politicians who have made the situation worse with their inflammatory comments. I have investigated racism in Wales as another vehicle of hostility towards outsiders and in particular, the events surrounding the KKK Grand Wizard Allan Beshella of Maesteg and the hate filled days of the 90's. I then look at the football hooligan firms of Wales, Cardiff, Newport, Wrexham and Swansea. I have gathered many stories from the lads involved and graphic tales of battles they've been involved in at home and abroad. I explain how these mobs often have to be segregated at Welsh games giving a major headache to the police and football authorities. I give my opinion on some of the major mobs of England based on battles they have been involved in over the years with Welsh clubs and finally I ask, "What does the future hold for these hooligan gangs?"

This book contains graphic tales of violence and strong language. If you're likely to be shocked or offended by this, please don't read any further. Thank you.

Finally, if you are reading this as a police officer and are thinking of nicking me, please be aware I will say under caution "I made up the whole thing." Cheers.

Chapter Two
Fire Breathing Dragons

The history of Welsh Nationalism and opposition to English newcomers goes back a long way in time. Various groups have sprung up over the years and launched terror campaigns against the English and anyone seen as helping them to 'invade' Wales and erode the Welsh way of life.

The 1950's saw a hugely increased demand for water in Liverpool and district and the decision was taken, whether rightly or wrongly is outside the scope of this article, to flood the Tryweryn Valley. The valley was also called Cwm Celyn and the failure of many prominent MP's at the time to halt this plan obviously drove some locals to direct action of the explosive variety. In 1969, two members of Muddiad Amddyfin Cymru [MAC] (Movement to defend Wales) died when a device they were carrying exploded. It is alleged that they were transporting the device to blow up a train which would be taking Prince Charles to his Investiture at Caernarvon. First founded and became active in the early 60's, this group was founded and led by John Jenkins. He was at the time a sergeant in the British Army in the Royal Army Dental Corps, RADC. They carried out and claimed responsibility for many bomb attacks including a blast at the GPO sorting office in Cowbridge Rd, Cardiff and another at left luggage at Cardiff Central train station.

Apart from the two members who died, other successes against MAC by the security services and the police were the conviction and jailing in 1966 of three more members of MAC. This was for blowing up installations and property to be used in the creation of the dam at Cwm Celyn. This was where a whole Welsh town was deliberately flooded to make a reservoir for the Scousers and wound up a lot of Welsh people. Then in 1970, MAC's leader, John Jones was jailed for 10 years and a fellow member, Frederick Alder was jailed for six years. They were both from Wrexham and were convicted of offences of conspiracy to cause explosions in Wales between 1966 and 1969. Today this group is inactive and would appear to have been destroyed.

From Bombs to Arson attacks

From bombings, these groups moved to arson attacks, starting in December 1979. They gave their justification as the shortage of affordable homes in North Wales for local people and the threat to the Welsh language and culture which the influx of English people represented. This was the year that **Meibion Glyndwr – The Sons of Glyndwr** first appeared. Meibion Glyndwr began burning property in December 1979 in protest at what it claimed was a growing trend of homes in rural Wales being sold as holiday cottages to people from England. This campaign went on well into the 90's and over 220 holiday homes were torched as well as boats, caravans and cars. In 1989, the group announced that 'every white settler' was a target for their campaign. In the 80's, the comedy show 'Not the Nine O'Clock News' did a spoof advert which showed a cottage burning and said "Come home to a REAL fire, buy a cottage in Wales." Only one person has ever been convicted of these attacks, namely Sion Aubrey Roberts who was jailed in 1993 for posting letter bombs to MP's and Estate Agents selling homes to English people. Police say that due to the remote location of a lot of these cottages and the obviously large number of small groups involved, catching them in the act was very difficult. Legend has it that MI5 were responsible for many of the attacks in an attempt to discredit Welsh Nationalist groups. This has never been proven however. The fact is that many people who could not afford housing particularly in these Welsh speaking communities and allegedly, many police officers were sympathetic to the campaign and turned a blind eye or refused to help investigators.

Running alongside these arson and letter-bomb campaigns, was the Free Wales Army (FWA) and Welsh Language activists who, demanding bilingual road signs, went on the rampage around Wales, ripping down and spray-painting signs until they had their own way. These same people also co-ordinated a Wales wide campaign of super-gluing cashpoint machines in order to force the banks to have bilingual instructions on the screen.

Meibion Glyndwr's campaign died out in the mid 90's due to the establishment of the Welsh Assembly although there have been numerous incidents since. These are generally blamed on copycats. A 61 year old man was jailed in 2001 for planting a fake bomb at the Assembly and **The Wales on Sunday** recently reported a growing number of paint attacks on English peoples' cars and second homes in which the initials 'MG' were used. The police have also recently announced they will be re-opening the holiday home arson investigation, using new DNA techniques. They could be opening a whole new can of worms if they do.

The anti-English hatred and chanting at Cardiff City matches is legendary and has been described in many books and articles. This will hopefully go some way to explaining the historical roots of this hate.

Chapter Three
Anti-English League

In the 80's, Exeter's firm had calling cards with 'Anti Welsh League' on them. Every time Welsh teams play the English, the chanting is mental. 'If you all hate England, clap your hands', 'Always shit on the English side of the bridge', 'Oh Engeeerland is full of shit, oh Engeeerland is full of shit, it's full of shit, shit and more shit, oh Engeeerland is full of shit'. These are just a few of the chants you will hear. The press call this 'racist' chanting and the police have nicked quite a few people for it under anti-racism laws. This is how ridiculous it's getting. They are trying to stamp out a tradition of anti-English hatred and banter that goes back many, many years and it ain't gonna be easy.

In the late 90's, author **AA Gill** branded the Welsh people 'ugly pugnacious little trolls'. A Swansea Councillor, Ioan Richard, demanded that he be prosecuted, saying "if these comments were made about black or Asian people then he would have been locked up by now". Interestingly, the Crown Prosecution Service (CPS) refused to prosecute him saying that although his language may have been insulting, it was not intended to stir up racial hatred. This is a very interesting legal point because according to the law, **'A Racist Incident is any incident which is perceived to be racist by the victim or any other person'**. Plenty of Welsh people perceived this as racist but the CPS did nothing. Obviously this law is not for Welsh people then. Another reason to hate the English.

In 1999, Welsh Language Party 'Plaid Cymru' called for local authorities in Wales to be given powers to restrict the purchase of second homes in Wales by English people as it increases house prices and drives people away from their communities because they can't afford housing. In 2001, the former Head of the Welsh Language Board, John Elfed Jones, was reported for prosecution to the Commission for Racial Equality after he said the effect of English migration into Wales was as damaging as foot and mouth disease. In 2001 another Councillor, Seimon Glyn of Gywnedd's Housing Committee told BBC Radio Wales that English was a 'foreign language' and said retiring English people moving to Wales were a 'drain on resources'.

Mike Parker, who co-wrote the Rough Guide to Wales book, said in Planet Magazine that English people moving to Wales are 'out and out racists'. He said their main motivation for moving to Wales was to 'get away from multi-cultural society and from black and Asian people in particular'. He added that they see rural Wales with its largely white population as a 'safe haven'. Even **Posh and Beckham** were told in 1998 to 'Stay away' after a Welsh Nationalist group, the **Welsh Language Society**, found out they had bought a holiday home in North Wales. Their spokesman, Gareth Kiff, said the protest would be secret but non-violent. According to the papers, their action often involves daubing property with slogans.

Many English people in these remote communities complain that many Welsh people blatantly speak Welsh in front of them and ignore them. Recently Welsh Language TV Presenter, Beca Brown, told Barn Magazine that she is racist and hates the English. Former UK Journalist of the Year, Miss Brown said, "If there was such a thing as Racists Anonymous, I'd go there and say I'm Beca, I'm Welsh and I'm racist." She also said, "I hate the English because they're English. It's as simple as that. We all know the English hate the Welsh and the Welsh hate the English. It's high time we told the truth."

Many English people have in the last few years moved to Wales. The newspapers have called it 'White Flight', saying many of them are moving from cities which are being flooded with asylum seekers and they see Wales as a safe haven. Don't know whether this is true or not but we've all noticed the many English accents in our midst in recent years and see people wearing all manner of English football tops around the place. It's a well known fact among older people round here that if you walked around here in any English football top in the 70's and especially the 80's, you would have been harassed in the streets and even attacked. It's not like that now and seems to have calmed down a lot. Many people don't seem to care nowadays, a sign of changing attitudes? Or is it just because there are cameras everywhere?

From the time the Cwm Celyn fiasco happened, right up until today, the hate continues. The Wales on Sunday recently reported a rise in anti-English graffiti and a Cardiff couple who bought some stables in West Wales found it daubed with anti-English graffiti. It said 'Cai Maes Sis' which is old Welsh for 'English Out'. The same idiot also injured one of their horses by stabbing it in the nose. This hatred is so endemic in Wales that it inevitably comes out when Welsh football teams play and especially when they play the English Clubs.

Will it ever end?

Chapter Four
The Barry Seaside Crew

I was born on Barry Island, a large town ten miles outside of Cardiff which once was home to the Butlins Holiday Camp, famous fairground and the busy Docks. Barry is a town with a history of violence and growing up, all my role models were thugs. The Island was famous for attracting gangs from all over the place including the Hell's Angel gang who, after a serious hiding from the locals, had petrol bombed the Pelican Club making national headlines. As a kid I used to witness mass brawls whilst walking my dog or sitting on the pub steps with my bottle of coke and bag of crisps. I really wanted to be a part of it.

I became a Punk in my early teens and then went on to become a Skinhead at age 15. By this age I was a fully fledged thug and due to the battles we used to have with naughty kids from the Thomas O'Beckett homes who used to stay at the holiday camp, I was well used to gang violence by this age. We used to travel into Cardiff on Saturdays and have running battles with the Mods and on Bank holidays and all summer we would fight down the Island with the Mods, Teds, Bikers, Asians; anyone who wanted to know.

Most days there would be around 40-50 boys we knew hanging around the fair or the camp but on Bank Holidays this would swell to 100-150 as all the Barry gangs, Colcot, Barry Dock, Bellites, Gibby Boys, Caddy Skins and Alexander Park crew would all descend on the Island in the hope of a row.

Mod Wars
Mods would come from far and wide to the Island, most famously the **Ponty Mods**, who came one time and mobbed up to about 200 in number and a massive battle kicked off on the beach. Families scattered as Punks, Skins and other Barry boys battled with Mods and rained pebbles down on each other and snapped up deckchairs to use as weapons. The Mods were using their crash-helmets as weapons and bodies were scattered all over the beach as the fighting raged on for about 15-20 minutes. The police who were first on the scene were bombarded with rocks and forced to make a sharp exit. Lone Mods who had been cut off from the main group disappeared under a hail of blows and Dr Martin boots. Despite the ferocity of this battle and the number of injuries, the boys who found themselves in front

of the courts were fined the massive sum of £20 with £2 court costs. Imagine what you'd get today? Two years jail, if you are lucky!

Mob Rule

We discovered that if a large group of people rock a wall (or railings), it doesn't matter how strong that wall is, if there are enough of you, it will go over. Thirty or more of us used to rock walls, some of them really long and over they'd go. The police must have been baffled by this wondering how all these walls were just 'falling down'. We left whole areas looking like they'd been bombed. When battles went off, the first thing to do would be to rip down a wall to use as ammo.

Scousers

A few of us were in the fairground one night and some local youngsters came running over saying that these Scousers were mouthing off up by the Butlin's entrance. We ran up to them and as I was arguing with them, I noticed one of them had a flick knife opened and was hiding it behind his leg. As I went for him, he pointed it at me saying "Get back soft lad." I could see from his eyes that he was crapping himself but I still didn't fancy getting stabbed so it was a standoff. Now when this argument had started there were around 10 of them and 10 of us but as every second passed, more and more of our boys were running up through the fair as word spread and now we had around 20 boys and some of ours were running up with metal poles, etc. They really didn't know what had hit them as they were battered from all sides with bottles, bricks, dustbin lids and brutally kicked unconscious. The few that escaped from us were caught by Brad, Cornwall and a few others and dealt a few slaps.

What these morons who came to the Island bullying kids didn't seem to understand was that, although we were spread out doing our own thing like chatting up birds or whatever, any sign of trouble and we would immediately mob up and batter them. This sort of thing happened regularly. A regular feature of the Skinhead days which became frowned upon when the Football Casuals evolved, was large gangs kicking shit out of one person. This used to happen all the time in those days. Although I condemn this behaviour as cowardly, I must admit that I did used to join in with these sort of attacks when I was a teenager. As I grew older, I realised that it's out of order and doesn't gain you any respect. It just makes you look like cunts. It's something the Swansea Jacks are famous for as well but we'll discuss them later.

I fucking hated the Scousers. We were always getting into scraps with them. They were the first ones I ever saw with the bowl type haircuts and casual gear and they always wanted to fight us. Fair play to them, they were game and we lost a few fights to them in the early days. When I say Scousers, I don't know if they were Liverpool or Everton at the time, we just used to hear that horrible accent and get into them.

Mugsy gets sliced

One night on the Causeway, Mugsy and a few of the Skins followed two guys with the intention of giving them a kicking. As Mugsy turned the one guy around to smack him, the guy sticks a butterfly knife straight through Mugsy's neck. As blood squirted all over the place, Jetley head-butts the knife man and Tater slams a rock into his head, knocking him clean out. The Old Bill arrived and rushed Mugsy to hospital where he was told it had missed his jugular by centimetres. Lucky! The stabber later had 6 months jail for this. If this happened nowadays, he would have had a lot longer.

A Bridge too far

One Bank holiday five of us stood on the railway bridge and a group of four Mods walked across. Hobbsy says "Lets have it" and kicks one of them down the steps while me, Packy and the others bash and stamp the fuck out of them. Hobbsy was half the size of the one he had kicked down the stairs and watching them fighting was hilarious. Hobbsy was kicking shit out of him but he wouldn't fight back as we were all stood there. Well funny. The train station bridge was a top place for ambushes for many years.

Me and my mate Barry were like a two man hit squad down the Island. We used to wander about some days looking for two strangers to bash. One day we jumped two Punks on the promenade and I knocked one out and Barry was doing the other one. I was just stood there and the one I had hit was getting up. Barry shouts, "Do him Jeff" and I volleyed him in the face with my Doc Martins, caning him right in. A few months later my sister was visiting relatives in Maerdy and she met these boys who said, "You're from Barry, are you? We got beat up by a kid called Jeff down there." Small world eh?

It ended up with me and Barry bashing a Mod from Cwmbran and taking his teeth out. We went to court and had a final warning that if we did it again, we'd find ourselves in a young offenders institution. Barry took the warning and vanished from the scene but did I? Did I fuck! Next Bank Holiday comes and there I am, in my Fred Perry T-shirt and braces with my Doc Martins on, looking for a scrap.

Butlins

As we approached pub-going age, we started climbing the fence to get into the Butlins Camp. As well as the fact that the place was crawling with birds, it was also attracting gangs of boys from far away who were obviously supporters of other football teams. We would be in the disco and someone would announce, "Those guys over there are Birmingham." Before you knew it, fists, feet and glasses would be flying. The security guards hated us in the Skinhead days as we were always kicking off and a lot of people were getting hurt. It was getting them a bad name. So we agreed with them that where possible, we would ambush anyone who started outside so as not to bring trouble to the guards. We used to ignore the stares of wankers who wanted trouble, drift outside in twos and threes, then ambush them up by the chalets. This drama was played out hundreds of times and worked really well. By the time they left they would usually be hanging drunk. We would not have had a drink at all and would destroy them.

Birth of the Casual

All of a sudden, the Skinhead look started disappearing and the Casual look was coming in. Bowl haircuts, Tachini tracksuits, Pringle jumpers and Adidas trainers were the new uniform of the hooligan. Suddenly thugs didn't look like thugs. They looked like the boy next door. This had the police totally baffled. They had this stereotypical image of the bovver boot wearing skinhead to look out for and these baby faced casuals were free to roam the streets and do what they wanted.

Now, as well as the football which we had started getting into, we had Butlins as a never ending battleground with other gangs. It was so cheap to go on holiday there that coaches full of people from Manchester, Liverpool, the Midlands, Yorkshire, Scotland, everywhere would turn up. Our mob was growing by the day as Cardiff, Dinas, Penarth, Sully and many other little teams we met at the football used to come down to drink with us. We never got done in there except on nights when only a few of us were out. If all our boys were there, we were unstoppable. One night I was in the disco talking to some birds and Coddy comes over and says some Scousers were starting on him. For some reason there were only about seven of us there. We put beer glasses inside our coats and went outside to wait for them. When they came out, there were about 40 of them and they were all massive compared to us. One of them said, "You sheep got a problem," and I said, "No." As I said it, the pint mug I had inside my jacket fell on the floor and smashed. The Scousers all roared with laughter and walked off. I was fucking fuming. I didn't like English getting away with liberties on our turf but if we had had a go there, we would have been murdered. You've gotta know when to bite your tongue if you wanna stay alive in this game.

Some others weren't so lucky though and large groups of Leeds, Millwall, Chelsea, Arsenal, various Mancs and other Northern bastards all came unstuck along Yellow Camp as we executed our ambushes. Some nights there with 50-60 of us, all tooled up with knuckledusters, bricks and bottles. The music in the disco was shocking, Shaka Khan, Salt and Pepper, Mel and Kim, Bros, A-Ha, Betty Boo, etc, but it all brings back memories of these top days when I hear them on 80's shows. Not a single day went by in Butlins where something didn't kick off. The number of people who were bashed, glassed or stabbed in there is unbelievable and could never happen on such a scale these days.

The Front

As well as the Camp, the nightclubs along the seafront were known as top places to get into a brawl especially at the Feathers because stag nights would come from near and far. One night I was stood in the doorway of the Beer Keller and I could see a mass brawl heading my way. 50 or 60 people engaged in fisticuffs and another 40 odd running around screaming, trying to break it up. Birds were screaming and fighting. It was mayhem. I thought, this is fuck all to do with me so I'll just watch. I saw this guy laying against a wall with 3 or 4 guys booting shit into him. As they moved off and he rolled over, I realised it was my mate Bear. I picked him up and took him inside, covered in blood as the fight raged on further down the road. In those days, the police used to drive past, go around the block and come back to arrest the survivors.

Same thing happened one night when I was stood in the Crop Chip shop and I saw a mass brawl coming across the road towards the shop. Fanos the owner, hurdles the counter and locks the door and then I see a mate of mine, Miller, getting his head booted against the glass time and time again. I came out and picked him up and took him home. Both of his eyes were so swollen he couldn't see at all. He was in a right state. These kind of fights were so common no-one seemed to bat an eyelid. With no CCTV hardly anyone used to get nicked and the police as I said, used to just think 'if you silly bastards wanna bash each other up, carry on'.

Ambush Alley

The tourists used to come out of Butlins and walk to the Crop Chip shop around 2:00am. Little did they know that we called this 'Ambush Alley'. This was where we used to sit around waiting for football boys to walk past. It would be like, "Where you from boys?" "Leeds" (or wherever) and we would just steam into them from all angles.

'W' tells of one bad incident on this road

"Me and S were walking up towards the Camp when two Mancs who were walking down the other way shouted, "Oi wankers," to us from the other side of the road. As I was saying, "You what?" S ran into the train station and came running back out and suddenly laid into them with some sort of bar. I joined in kicking them as he beat them both savagely around the head with this object. I sat up all night shitting myself that he had killed them because when we ran off, they were both in a bad way. I called for him and said, "Where's the tool?" He said he had thrown it in the park so I made him go and get it. I was sure this would be a murder enquiry but amazingly we never heard anything again. Thank God.

As the 80's was moving on, the violence was getting worse and knifings were happening all over the place. As a result, a lot of us started carrying blades. You begin to think that if they use blades, so will we and it becomes a vicious circle. Instead of just bashing people up now, we were slashing them across the arse or face and this also happened to a few of our boys too. It was getting out of hand for a while.

It was outside the Crop that I eventually ended up stabbing two Mancs and getting a two year stretch in Her Majesty's Hotel as I explained fully in my first book. While I was inside, I missed out on loads of good scraps including the Wales – Germany game in Cardiff which was mental. I was gutted not to be there to have a go at those German bastards. When I came out, I was straight back into the scene and within about a week, I was involved in a massive affray with some English idiots. Not long after this in 1991, we travelled down to Swansea and went on the rampage. I was back. Even though I ended up inside three times during these years, I don't regret a single thing. It was the best time of my life and I loved it.

Further reading :
'Soul Crew Seasiders' by Jeff Marsh available from www.lulu.com/uk

Chapter Five
The Swansea Jacks

Swansea is around fifty miles west of Cardiff and is home to our sworn enemies known as 'The Jacks'. The hatred between the two clubs is legendary and goes back many, many years. The Jacks have had a large hooligan following at home since the 80's and are still very active today. Every time a local derby occurs between Swansea and Cardiff, there is major trouble. In his book, Swansea's self appointed 'top boy' Andrew Tooze claims that every time they have played Cardiff, they have battered or chased the Cardiff fans. He says Cardiff are the 'Man United of Wales' meaning they have a lot of boys from all over the place but run at the first sign of trouble.

The thing is with these games, there are so many incidents all over the place involving small groups that it's hard to say if some of these things did happen or did not. They may have bashed or chased some Cardiff but I can say in my experience I have never been in an incident involving Swansea where my group have been battered or run although I have felt my arse go once or twice in these battles. In no way have Cardiff's main firm ever been done by them as their book claims. In my opinion, they have a tight 50-100 boys who stick together and are hard to shift at home and have a loose mob of around 200 but their away mob is not as fantastic as they seem to think. Tooze is known as 'Steroid come lately' seeing as he's a big steroided up geezer who admits he's only been actively involved with the Jacks firm since 2000. He's become involved at a time where most places you go, you get a massive police escort and can have adventures with very little danger of actually getting battered. So a lot of the cunts who go to football these days, in a lot of clubs, are Stone Island wearing wankers who turn up at places like Millwall or West Ham and give it the big 'un behind the police lines and then go home saying, "I went there, fucking mugs." A lot of the new breed of Hooligans (Tooze included) wouldn't have lasted 5 minutes in the 80's and that's a fact.

The South Wales Evening Post in the 80's talks about two bank holiday rows involving the Jacks. One was at a 'point to point' horse race meeting in Brecon in which 60 Swansea and Merthyr boys fought for two hours before it was finally stopped. The other was an affray at the Quadrant pub in Swansea after 100 Cardiff lads (mainly from Neath and Port Talbot) took over their pub. The Jacks had attacked and put a few windows through before the Old Bill had turned up and arrested a load of them, saving them from being massacred. Battles between Swansea and Cardiff happen all over South Wales in Clubs, pubs, on beaches, anywhere they happen to meet, such is the intense hatred between the two.

Swansea v Crystal Palace played at Ninian Park in the early 80's. After the game as Swansea fans were making their way from the ground having had various battles with Cardiff fans, a van full of Crystal Palace fans pulled up and attacked the Jacks, stabbing one of them to death. A 19 year old Cockney received a life sentence for this.

The Swansea Jacks book by Tooze and Wallis

It has to be said that this book bears little resemblance to the reality of the war between the Jacks and Cardiff over the years. On reading this book you would think the roles had been reversed and that Swansea were the ones with the massive mob that wins most of its battles due to its large numbers and the calibre of its main boys. The book is full of lies and distortions from beginning to end which is a shame as it could have been a good read. Wallis describes the time that Cardiff ambushed them by the Ninian pub which I wrote about in my first book. According to him, we attacked from all sides but the Jacks held firm. This is clearly rubbish - even the Jacks who were there that day must surely know that! After we pulled a wall down and attacked their much larger numbers, they erupted into panic and scattered. I've no idea if they were attacked from behind at the same time as we were chased away after a scuffle with the police. Out of approximately 200 Jacks, I would say I saw around 10 that seemed willing to stay and have a go. The rest were like scared rabbits who didn't know what to do. The Jacks have a bad reputation for cowardly attacks on small groups and innocents. Once they land in Cardiff, they will literally attack anyone and this is well documented. Like the time they attacked the gay bar and the Owain Glyndwr incident. In the book, it says they stormed into the Owain screaming, "Jack Army" and sprayed Cardiff's 'lads' with ammonia and battered them. The Owain has never been a football boys' pub. It's simply too far from the ground. One of the guys in the pub (Alan) at the time tells his version of what happened:

"Picture the scene: Cardiff City v Swansea City 1992-3 ish. Me and four mates were drinking at 5:30pm at the Owain Glyndwr in Cardiff Centre. Because of refurbishment, there was only one way in and out. The other door was closed. Only 12-14 people approximately in the pub at this time. Suddenly 50 Jack bastards stormed the pub. They punched my mate in the head who was knocked out but finally managed to stagger his way out via the women's toilets (there was an emergency exit in there). They beat up the bouncer, gave the bar staff a good kicking (women), sprayed ammonia in women's faces before giving them a kicking for fun. Luckily my mate threw a chair through the window and we all legged it. This is why I hate the Jacks. They didn't have the balls to go to Canton for a fight but chose a pub in town with only 12 people in there. On top of all that for good fun, they beat up women too."

Doesn't sound as good when you hear this side of the argument does it? Wallis also goes on to claim that 30 five Jacks ran hundreds of Cardiff in Sloper road (outside the ground) and says things like, "We ran up the road and as usual Cardiff's mob were nowhere." This guy must be on drugs. Everyone knows if we play Swansea, every thug from miles around, even hordes of boys who are nothing to do with football come out of the woodwork. The only way this would happen is if they (as they did in '93) turn up when everyone's already in the ground and they then get away with bashing stragglers.

Their other great 'result' was when they turned up unexpectedly at the Exchange in Canton. According to Stretch Armstrong, Tooze entered the pub and knocked out two of Cardiff's main boys. Well, the boys who were there tell a different story. They charged in giving it the big 'un, smashed a few things, hit a punter who was not football then ran up the street as Cardiff chased and battered them. If you want proof of this, see the video of the Exchange incident on www.vsocial. com/video/?d=19541. In fact the guy they supposedly knocked out is clearly seen running after them and attacking them for which he was later nicked.

More evidence of their willingness to batter people who are on their own is evidenced by looking at the small print of a newspaper article entitled 'Soccer Insanity' in the book. It says that a youngster needed stitches in his eye and lost four teeth after being attacked by 20 Swansea fans. This book is worth a look, if only for comedy value, but is so full of lies that any Jack who was actually there through all those years must be cringing with embarrassment.

Newspaper article about Swansea versus Cardiff.
"Not exactly a football fixture to get the pulses racing, is it? With the oval ball, maybe. Definitely not with the round one. Unless of course, you actually come from Swansea or Cardiff in which case you will be practically hyperventilating. The Old Firm derby in Glasgow or its north London equivalent or the famous one on Merseyside are just meaningless kick-abouts compared to this. Swansea City v Cardiff City is the mother of all derbies. On the field it is pretty committed but in the stands, it is

positively apocalyptic. After their 89th minute winner yesterday, the 6,000 Swansea fans were delirious. They jumped and jeered at their rival supporters caged in behind the goal, chanting, "We beat the scum 2-1," instantly forgetting they had been 1-0 down for much of the match. In the past, ugly scenes would have ensued but the police are wise to this now and were there in force. Beneath the throb of hovering helicopters, they ushered 1,500 stunned Cardiff fans into their waiting coaches and back whence they came. The essence of this encounter is not so much keeping up with the Jones's as murdering them. Among the fans, violence is not only possible, it's compulsory. This is the game's last bastion of regular crowd trouble. It's all John Toshack's fault. If he hadn't rejuvenated Swansea in the late 70's, the cream of South Wales football would never have met on the same pitch. Cardiff were always a division or two above but suddenly they were on a par and Swansea were getting the plaudits. The fact that Toshack was a Cardiff boy just added further insult.

Emotions which ran high throughout the Eighties, boiled over when the two sides met in the FA Cup first round in 1991. Swansea won the match 2-1 and chaos broke out. Supporters showered each other with bricks, stones and metal from a nearby building site and Swansea City centre resembled a Brighton seafront battle in Quadrophenia. Swansea fans took revenge at Ninian Park two years later, just before Christmas. A pitch invasion delayed the start by 40 minutes and having beaten Swansea 1-0 in the League, they ripped up seats and wood from the stand and went on the rampage. They really meant harm. "It was carnage," remembers one local journalist. "We were ducking down in the press box." There were many injuries and arrests. Front page headlines like 'Season of Hatred' and 'Night of Defeat and Destruction' said it all.

For the next four years, visiting supporters were banned from the match at either venue. They were allowed back in controlled numbers last season but team mascots, Barclay the Bluebird and Cyril the Swan, are banned in case they exacerbate the situation. Yesterday, Cardiff fans wishing to attend the match were obliged to congregate at their own ground by 9am. There they were herded onto 40 coaches for the hour's journey west. Police cars and outriders cordoned off all roads and flanked the convoy to allow it to snake its way to Swansea unhampered. To complete the Orwellian scene, a helicopter escorted the coaches and police guarded bridges and roundabouts. There were pockets of Swansea fans to taunt with, "You Jack bastards" en route, but all streets around the ground were closed. The home supporters were already inside and as the convoy arrived local residents peered nervously through net curtains. Torrents of abuse were exchanged as soon as the visitors were hustled in and the Swansea contingent were soon into a rendition of "Swimaway, a-swimaway" accompanied by breaststroke motions. This is a reference to some Cardiff faithful pitching into the sea one year to escape their Swansea pursuers.

No one is quite sure where this animosity stems from. Cardiff people say Swansea 'Jacks' have a chip on their shoulder and do not actively support the Welsh team. Swansea men see their Cardiff counterparts as privileged and soft. They have a damning way of saying 'pathetic' and 'tart'. They sent some provocative emails to the Cardiff City website last week with gang threats and warnings to be 'tooled up or else'. There is still a sad bunch who pride themselves on being hard. Thankfully, the event passed off without major incident. Perhaps the pitiful standard of play helped: the ball spent most of its time in the air. The fans would have been united in their misery but for Swansea's last-minute winner scored by an Englishman. If Swansea win the return in April, they will be the first team to do the Welsh 'double'. Such is the abrasive nature of this fixture."

Some Jacks' accounts of battles they've been involved in over the years
S's Story
"My first away game with Swansea was Millwall away in the mid 80's. On the way up I couldn't see what all the fuss was about. About 70 of us went in their end and at this stage I still wasn't worried. As we entered the stand and started singing 'Swansea', the whole end just steamed into us. They kicked and battered us all around the place. We were literally fighting for our lives in there. After a good 15-20 minutes of battling with the Old Bill not giving a shit about trying to help us, we eventually got out of there. What a relief I can tell you. Millwall were like savages trying to get to us throughout the game. I was really thinking, 'this is it, we're going to die here'. Luckily after the game, Millwall had all run off up to the station to ambush us so we climbed on our coach and got the hell out of there with no further problems. If we had come by train, I reckon we would have died that day - it was that dodgy. One of the Swans boys who was only 18 died a few days later from a brain haemorrhage after taking a load of kicks to the head at Millwall. That's why we always turn out for them, to avenge our fallen comrade."

Exeter v Swansea 1990 by JA
"Exeter had a good mob back in the 80's but since then they've become a bit of a joke. Around 1990 we played them down there and there were a few scuffles around the place. We wanted them to be mobbed up as their 'Anti Welsh League' calling cards and chants are legendary. We really wanted to give it to them. Although they had loads of fans, they only had about 15-20 proper lads and they all seemed really

young to me. They call themselves the Sly Crew these days but they're not much of a crew at all. A kiddy firm is what they are."

Swansea v Panathinaikos

Fighting in a bar led to ten Jacks being locked up although they were eventually allowed to buy their way out of prison. The Jacks however, claimed they were fighting for their lives as hordes of locals attacked the bar with tools. It's often the case abroad that the police let the locals get away with murder and nick the foreigners.

Millwall Tel's trip to Swansea

"We came out at Swansea train station to be faced with a mob of about 100-120 stone and bottle throwing chavs. To be honest, if it wasn't for the police presence, the Millwall that were there would have gone through them but fair play to them, it was like going back to the 80's coming out of the station to be confronted by a mob like that. Only other place that's happened lately to us is at Cardiff. I'd say there were a good 60 proper boys there, the rest were chavvy cunts but respect where it's due, they had a go which is more than a lot of people do."

A national newspaper article says that Swansea hooligans CS gassed police on a tube train whilst away to Millwall. Article also states that Swansea fans put up posters around Swansea asking everyone to go to Millwall and calling for 'no runners'. Something their critics would say was done to ensure that the police knew their intentions and they would get a guaranteed escort to Millwall.

Swansea and the Far Right

When I went to a game against Swansea at the end of the 90's. They had a mob of around 40 with BNP flags in the corner of the Grange end and many of them were Seig Heiling towards us. They think this upsets us as Cardiff have a lot of black followers. Most people really don't care a fuck and they must be brain dead if they don't think the police will film them doing this and eventually present it all to a court and get them banged up big time. Tooze has arranged several BNP meetings in Swansea and revelled in the bad publicity this gained him. Swansea player Lee Trundle showed the same Swansea mentality when he held up a flag which said "Fuck off Cardiff" after their victory over Carlisle at the Millennium Stadium which led to the muppet getting arrested.

News report about the Jacks BNP activities

"In Swansea, South Wales, 50 football hooligans gathered from 10:00am in the

NAME THIS THUG

The photograph that will shame football

Here's Nazi Jack Lee Wallis 'Seig Heiling' his way round Plymouth which cost him a lifetime ban.

Trundle's minder is a soccer thug

AND HE HAS BNP LINKS

EXCLUSIVE

THE bodyguard and close friend of shamed Swansea City soccer star Lee Trundle is a convicted soccer hooligan who has attended a major right-wing BNP party rally.

Top striker Trundle was arrested for displaying an obscene T-shirt and waving an offensive flag at rivals Cardiff City after his side lifted the Football League Trophy last weekend.

On Thursday, he and Swans defender Alan Tate were given a police caution for public order offences and still face a Football Association of Wales probe.

Battle

Now the News of the World has discovered his minder and friend Andrew Tooze, 39, was given a prison sentence after a pitched battle between fans before a Wales international in 2003.

More than 50 fans from Swansea, Cardiff and Newport clashed after booing in bars near the Milan ground.

Twenty-stone skinhead Tooze was found guilty of violent disorder and sentenced to 12 months' jail, suspended for a year. He was kicked out of Italy and didn't even see the match.

But Tooze, a security guard and weightlifter who also runs a coffee shop in Swansea, went on to become a close pal of Liverpool-born Trundle and claims to be his "unofficial minder".

Defended

He defended Trundle, saying he had merely picked up the flag and T-shirt thrown by supporters and held them up for a few seconds.

Father-of-four Tooze has also admitted attending a British National Party meeting in a Swansea church hall where its leader Nick Griffin was the main speaker.

But the former nightclub bouncer denied any other links to the BNP.

He said: "I wanted to hear what the BNP had to say but I decided they were talking a load of rubbish."

ON WATCH: Andrew Tooze (right) with Swansea City striker Lee Trundle

Mad Hatter club to watch the England match. Booked by Andrew Tooze, a BNP stalwart and body builder, the private function was also the launch pad for an attack on a 'Smash the BNP' concert in the City later that evening. Also organising on the day was Jason Ryan, one of the leaders of the 'Swansea Riot Squad' hooligan gang and an ardent racist. Ryan, who regular spills his racist bile on the Internet using the handle SRS, recently had a rape charge against him dropped for lack of evidence. By mid-afternoon, the drunken Swansea thugs began leaving the Mad Hatter for a pub closer to the café hosting the concert. Worried about potential trouble the police warned the café owner who, under their advice, cancelled the event."

The media love to paint all football hooligans as racists. It makes the story more exciting and gets the police more interested in busting you. If evidence can be presented to a court stating that not only are you a hooligan, you're also a Nazi, you are going away for a long time (like Mariner and Frayne, the Chelsea Headhunters). There are undoubtedly a lot of racists in every mob but most of them keep it to themselves. Maybe Swansea are so openly racist that they have been humiliated and hurt so many times by Cardiff and more particularly the Docks boys, many of whom are black. In the rave days, one of the Docks boys even chased the Jacks with a pistol and quite a few Jacks have been carved up by the Docks boys who are terrible blade merchants and used to call themselves 'Docks Machete Crew'. This could be the reason then. Who knows?

Here are some Jacks' versions of rows they've been involved in over the years.

S's version of Barry Town – Swansea '84
"Not many Jacks made the trip to Barry and when they did arrive, they wished they hadn't bothered as 150-200 scum (Cardiff) turned up and chased the handful of Jacks that were there all round the crappy ground. One idiot was even waving a Stanley knife around. We took a fair few digs and kicks as we finally escaped from the ground. What a buzz to get out of there in one piece. Mind you, if we had our mob there it would have been a different story"

One of the Jacks, 'J' relates some of the trips he's experienced
"Where do I start? I've been following Swansea since I was a little kid. The best games for me have always been the derbies against Cardiff who we lovingly call 'The Scum'. We ran the Scum at the Quadrant one time and it was the best feeling of my life to see the bastards running and shitting themselves as bricks whizzed past their heads. We haven't always had it all our own way mind and I've been to Cardiff and been terrified as our small group of around 50 tried to get to the

ground as hordes of Scum came at us from everywhere. This was late 80's and I never thought I was gonna get out of it alive. Swings and roundabouts though innit? I still say we've had more results against Scum than they've had with us and I'd put our main 50 against Scum's main 50 anytime and you know there'd only be one winner.

The other Welsh firms are always a guaranteed ruck because us Taffies are born to fight and when we meet there's always a top tear up. Taking the fight to the English is the next best feeling. When the adrenaline starts pumping, there's no better drug on this planet. When we played Torquay, although they had no football mob as such, we still had a top time. They had loads of game lads in the pubs and we done all-comers and totally wrecked the place. Bristol Rovers away was another good trip although we legged them everywhere. When the game was on, 50 or more of them terrorised five of our youngsters and chased them into a Paki shop and gassed them. Very brave boys! Shame they didn't want to know when we were mobbed up. When we heard they had done this, we steamed one of their pubs and they went out the back door, leaving stragglers to take the revenge beating. I used to have respect for the Worzels but after that little performance we show them no mercy now.

Chester have a tidy little firm, 'The 125's'. They only have around 30-40 proper boys but a few times our lads have clashed with them and they deserve a mention as they are totally game. Oldham deserve a mention too as another crew without massive numbers but who are always there and try to have a go.

Lincoln City's 'Transit Elite' had a good effort a few years ago but we smashed them all over their city. We only had around 40 lads to their 100. After a very violent confrontation in which a few lads got bloodied on both sides, we chased them back into their pub and wrecked the place. Respect goes out to them but they were totally shocked by the ferocity of the SRS (Swansea Riot Squad).

Hull away around 2001 was a lively trip although the police had it sewn up really. Around 100 of us turned up early doors at Goole, a few miles away. We phoned the Hull boys and arranged a meet. When we got off at Hull though, we were met by hundreds of robocops. As we were escorted past these shitty high rise flats, about 100 of them attacked the escort. The Old Bill went berserk, battering loads of boys on both sides and it was all over. Respect to Hull. They were up for it. It's just a shame that the Old Bill were on top or that would have been a wicked row. The newspapers said we were battling with baseball bats but I never saw any. It's just more media bullshit making us look bad. The only tools I saw used that day were the police tooling us.

The best games of all time for me though, apart from the old scum games of course were Bristol City at our place where the police dog lost an eye (fuck him) and Millwall when they came and we really showed them a 'Welcome in the Hillsides'. I'm sure the Worzels and the Cockneys got more respect for us after those games."

NCIS report of Merthyr Tydfil v Swansea

15 minutes after the start of the game, a group of around 12 Swansea fans left the ground and went to a lounge bar nearby. An hour later, a group of 35-40 Cardiff supporters made their way to the same bar and a confrontation took place. Police officers battled to move the Cardiff supporters away and one man was arrested after a struggle. Merthyr is a Cardiff stronghold and many good boys come from there. Oxford recently took 40 boys there unexpectedly and there was nobody there to confront them - all the lads were at a game in Cardiff. They don't realise how lucky they were. If it was known they were coming, they would have had the shock of their lives. They escaped with it that time.

When the Jacks pass through Cardiff Central, there is usually fun and games. Here's a press report of them on their way back from Shrewsbury a few years ago.
"A 250 strong mob of Swansea City supporters fought with police and wrecked a train at Cardiff Central station on their way back from their team's game at Shrewsbury on Saturday. Damage valued at around £10,000 was caused to two carriages of a First Great Western train which had to be taken out of service for repairs. Two people were arrested at the time but British Transport Police have set up Operation Thunderbird to track down more of the culprits. They are reviewing CCTV footage of the clashes which started when Cardiff City fans were spotted on different platforms. Dog handlers and officers from South Wales Police were called in to control the fans. Several BTP officers received facial injuries during the incident."

Rotherham - Swansea City

An inquiry has begun into the death of a Swansea City fan who died after being trampled and fatally injured by a police horse during clashes between rival fans. Swansea City supporter Terry Coles, 41, died in hospital after suffering a fractured skull and crush injuries before the Third Division championship decider at Rotherham. South Yorkshire Police Assistant Chief Constable Tim Hollis said the tragedy happened as rival supporters threw missiles at each other and about 100 Swansea fans were escorted to Rotherham's Millmoor Lane ground. Security video footage of the incidents showed people crouching against a wall outside the ground trying to escape the missiles. The police horse, one of three in the vicinity, was cantering down a slope to deal with the trouble when it collided with Mr Coles. "The victim had not seen the horse and he appeared to be walking into the line of the animal," said Mr Hollis. "It quite clearly rides over him." Police arrested 19 fans before the match which ended in a 1-1 draw, securing the title for Swansea. Play was stopped twice following pitch invasions after each goal. The arrested supporters have been charged with a variety of offences including affray and being drunk and disorderly. All 19, a mixture of Swansea and Rotherham fans, have been bailed to appear in court on 8-10 May. According to Jacks I've spoken to, Coles was not a 'boy', ie someone connected to a Casual Firm but what is known as a 'Barmy' which is a normal supporter who may play up when drunk. The police officer responsible got away with it and is free to do it again. Even a Jack doesn't deserve to die in this way so RIP Terry Coles.

Southend - Swansea 2000
From the News of the World (Welsh edition)
There was tension before the match when around 50 Swansea thugs invaded the West Bank Stand to confront Southend fans. Police and club stewards rushed to the scene when more of the 500-strong travelling Swansea contingent threatened to join in the punch up. The trouble lasted several minutes before police dispersed it and formed a cordon separating the two sets of supporters.

'SWANS FANS ARRESTED IN BIG MATCH TROUBLE'
From the South Wales Evening Post
Seven people were arrested and hundreds of pounds worth of damage caused in angry scenes involving Swans fans at the weekend. Police battled to keep opposing fans away from each other in the run up to Saturday's match between Plymouth Argyle and Swansea City. About 130 Swansea fans congregated in the Noah's Ark pub in Courtenay Street in the city centre before lunchtime and more than 80 officers from the tactical aid group were called to contain them. A hard core of supporters tried to break through the police lines but were forced back into the pub after a minor scuffle. A 27 year old man was arrested for disturbing the peace. At the same time, between 30 and 50 fans were causing havoc in the Britannia Inn, Milehouse. The Swans fans had arrived in the city by coach and train and were later escorted to the ground for the game that Plymouth won 1-0. There were minor scuffles on the way with Argyle supporters and one 31 year old Swansea man was

arrested for disorderly behaviour. There were further scuffles outside the ground, before and after the game, as police battled to keep control. Four others were also arrested on public order offences and were appearing in Plymouth Magistrates court today.

Swansea City v Wigan Athletic 12/08/00 - Nationwide League Division 2

Following this fixture, a group of 40 Swansea supporters made their way to a public house. On leaving the pub, some of the Swansea supporters came across a group of students. The Swansea group mistakenly thought the students were from Cardiff and attacked them. One of the students had a bottle smashed into the side of the head causing a wound that later required 40 stitches. The other seven all received injuries. The eight students eventually managed to escape and ran to a nearby pub pursued by the Swansea supporters. With the assistance of the staff, the doors to the pub were shut and locked preventing the pursuing mob from getting in. The Swansea supporters proceeded to smash every window in the pub with an array of missiles found nearby, resulting in several of the customers who were already in there being cut by flying glass, some later requiring stitches. Police arrived and five Swansea supporters were arrested for serious assault and criminal damage.

Swansea v Hull 2001

Swansea took around 100 lads and clashed with Hull fans all around the ground. Swansea were heavily outnumbered but according to reports put up a good fight.

Jinks (Cardiff lad) tells of his nightmare trip to Jackland

Don't know how to start it but it was the game where we were banned from going down there. It was a night match maybe around 94/95/96. We lost 4-1 I think.

Me and my mate Dion went down in his car for the game. It was a disaster from the start. After parking the car, we walked towards the Vetch and we had to pass a pub with 20 odd jacks outside. I said to my mate, "Pretend we know where we are going." The lads outside the pub were staring at us as we approached them but I think nerves got the better of us because I crossed the road and he went a different way then shouted, "Jinks hang on," and started following me. The Jacks were looking at us and talking amongst themselves and started following us but as we turned the corner, we were met by the sight of the Vetch and loads of police.

As we were going through the turnstiles, I noticed that we were still being followed by some of the lads from the pub and things went worse when a copper who me nor my mate knew said too loudly for our liking, "Oi, ain't you Cardiff fans?" Dion said, "Jinks we are fucked." We got into the ground. It was the second tier above the goals. We looked around for familiar Cardiff faces who said they were coming into this stand when we spoke to them during the week and the hundreds who clapped their hands when the 'If your all gonna Swansea, clap your hands' was sung at Ninian. It dawned on us that it was just us two and to make matters worse some of the lads from the pub we had passed were behind us - only about 6 to 8 of them but they were telling everyone who we were.

We didn't see any of the game. Every time Swansea scored, the Jacks jumped up and down celebrating and me and my mate just sat there. We didn't move and were subjected to getting covered in spit and having sly punches thrown at us from a few directions and getting called 'Cardiff scum'. We wanted to get out of there for ages but we would have been battered. Then, a minute or two from the end, three coppers came to us. One who I recognised as a Cardiff spotter called Barbara (Babs) told us to leave or be arrested. Me and Dion decided to go but I have to be honest, the thought of being arrested didn't sound too bad for the two of us.

We arrived outside the ground and started to walk in the direction we had come from. I looked around but the Jack lads were still in the ground. I said to Dion that Babs might have stopped them from following us out and we laughed at each other. We were safe. Then a few hundred yards in front of us, four or five lads came walking towards us. We stopped and a scruffy skinny lad came up to us and said, "We know who you are. Let's have it." They walked back up the street and stood on the corner. We were stunned but it was only a matter of time before the lads in the ground came out after us so we walked towards the four or five Jacks. They walked around the corner. As we approached the corner, the scruffy Jack came flying at us but was floored by Dion. The Jack stood up and ran off. His mates looked unsure of themselves although calling it on wasn't really doing much. Then I heard someone shout, "There they are." I looked and saw the scruffy Jack running towards us with what looked like about 30 lads following him. They were all over us. I was getting kicked and punched but because so many all wanted to have a punch or a kick, I think it helped as they all got in each other's way. I noticed Dion backing off so I shouted, "Run." I broke free, caught up with Dion and passed him. I turned around and it looked like there was now more joining the chase (so much for Toozey saying Cardiff are bullies in his book). I heard Dion shout, "Where we going?" I didn't know. I noticed a car coming out of a petrol station so I opened the door and jumped in. Dion jumped in the back but the bloke driving started shouting, "Take my money, take my money." I told him to shut the fuck up. I didn't want his money. I just wanted a lift and to drive like fuck as there were loads of Jacks looking for us. As he pulled out of the garage, I noticed the driver trying to cover his Swansea top by zipping up his jacket. There were loads of Jacks looking for us on the street corner but we ducked down. I hoped the driver wouldn't stop by them. They looked really mad that we had escaped and were bouncing. Fair play to the driver. He took us to where our car was parked. We were aching all over and bruised but how we got away I'll never know."

Dai's view of Sheffield Utd away 2007

350 Jacks made their way to Bramhall Lane to chants of, "Did the Ripper shag your Mam." Despite numerous threats from internet warriors, only minor scuffles took place and in all I thought they (Sheffield) were a big let down. My conclusion about the Jacks is, they have got a firm and they can do a bit of damage but I feel they come a poor second to Newport and Cardiff who are by far the best two firms in Wales. I find it hard to say anything nice about Swansea as I fucking hate them, however respect is due to them for the goes they had at Bristol City and Millwall down there - those two firms are no mugs. As the Jacks have gone up this year and we will soon be playing them again, most lads wouldn't bother going as it's a proper bubble game with massive police overkill and buses in and out the only mode of transport. Waste of time these days. Cardiff fans have even been banned from travelling to Swansea in the past and probably will be again. Good memories of the old days, gone forever. The hate will live on forever though and fights in the pubs and clubs around South Wales over this rivalry will never end.

Further reading :

'Swansea Jacks
- From Skinhead to Stone Island'
Published by Headhunter books.

Chapter Six
Newport County

During the 80's Newport had a good little firm but never called themselves anything. While most other clubs had names like Chelsea's 'Headhunters', Northampton's 'Affray Team', Leicester's 'Baby Squad', etc, Newport never bothered with names. These days their youth firm are known as the DYC (Disorderly Young Casuals) and are seemingly keeping the flag flying well. As Newport is only 15 minutes from Cardiff and is on the main train line from London, ourselves and Swansea fans often pass through there on the way to or from games as do the other teams playing us. During the 80's, we'd often be coming back from late games and as our train passed through the station, we'd be faced with around 100 Casuals trying to attack our train. As I explained in my other book, they had a lot of bottle and would often travel to Cardiff on non-match days and launch surprise attacks on our pubs. Not many others would have attempted that. Swansea have turned up at stupid times and terrorised innocent people but only once have they ever gone to a pub on a non-match day (The Exchange) and ended up being run everywhere. (See CCTV on youtube)

Dai's version of County's game against Merthyr, played at Ninian Park around 1987

"We must have had close to 500 lads who all travelled on our train - all the old lads out of retirement. We pushed straight past the Old Bill in Cardiff and run through the streets looking for Cardiff. A mob of Cardiff come running around the corner and see this massive mob of Newport coming. They turn on their heels and they are gone. We chased them to the Philharmonic and smashed all the windows and wrecked the joint. For the rest of the day, we clashed with loads of groups of Cardiff and did them every time. Even when they had a skip full of ammo and after they had finished throwing stuff, they ran. They were game and kept coming and coming and I'm sure they would say they did us but the truth is, we came out on top every time we met them. We had big numbers out that day and it still gives me satisfaction to know we terrorised the whole of Cardiff. At the replay a few days later, they had a better mob out and so did the police. Fifty of us legged it into the bus station and had a cracking toe-to-toe. No-one backed off and it went on for ages. The police couldn't stop it as they were busy holding back the rest of County's lads. Gotta give the Cardiff lads respect for turning out and having a go.

They made it a memorable occasion."

Brian explains life in Newport (once voted most violent town in Britain)
The DYC thing is the Disorderly Young Casuals, the tag 'Casuals' has stuck with the county boys for some time. As I said back in the mid 80's, I worked as a doorman at Lazers in Newport on Stow Hill which was once the Stow Away and has had numerous names, Brooklyn Heights, Zanzibar and now Escapade, I believe. A Friday and Saturday night would see 16 doormen working in a club that held 1000 punters. Some nights we needed 16, some nights were quiet (just a few scuffles).
I remember one Friday night in particular. I even remember the song playing at the time 'Tarzan Boy' by Baltimore! Lemmy (Newport's main football boy, now deceased) and about ten or so of the County boys started causing mayhem on the dance floor. Myself, Kevin from Ringland who was a scaffolder and Dai from Pontypool and also Liam from Somerton, all piled into them and had four of them in headlocks straight out through the emergency exit and into the car park behind the club. By this time, Rico, Harry, Alan and Coxy had arrived and we were in the car park having a good old scrap. Next thing, "Oi, you fuckers." It was Mike the club owner, a Cockney. He was out on the fire escape landing, "Get back inside," he screamed. He wiped the floor with us. "Chuck 'em out but no mass brawls in the car park please." The County boys hung out in the Hall of Fame pub in Newport as it was called. It looks out towards the entrance of Newport railway station and is very handy for spotting away fans arriving. The pub was once called the Greyhound for many years. At the time, the Hall of Fame was run by Trevor a former head doorman at the Stow Away, (Lazers etc.) and was not a man to be messed with. He still runs a pub in Newport, now called 'The Lamb' at the end of Bridge St. Trevor's brother was Dick Richardson 'the Maesglas Marciano'. Anyone who knows the history of British boxers will have heard of Dick. During that era one pub not to go in and look for a fight was the Friendship! It is on the Ringland council estate close to the Spencer Boys club where a certain young **Nathan Blake** was spotted.

Lemmy was a top lad, a likeable rogue you could say. He didn't deserve to die the way he did (explained later). The other main face at Newport was Tutty. He always went to Lazers on the weekends. He always wore all the trendy gear that they wore at the time. You could say he was the top dresser out of all the county boys from what I can remember. He and his brother were always in trouble with the Old Bill. Timmy Porter and Knobby Coldrick are another two of the old County crew and tidy lads they are too, just don't mess with them. If you are doing a piece on Newport, I think the Hartridge rugby boys from the Friendship in Ringland deserve a mention. Barko Wheeler, 41, is still playing rugby today for Newport Saracens and the rugby league team in Newport. He was attacked a while back with a sword just after one of the Ringland boys' funerals ('Spooky'). It was a similar type of sword to that which Lemmy met his death with. Barko was stabbed in the throat area and was very lucky to survive. Mark Wheeler from Ringland and Sammy Sims (Steve, he was British boxing champion at lightweight I think), after retiring during the 80's, ran a few pubs in the town, the Welsh Prince at the bottom of Commercial St being one. Last time I saw Sammy was on the Bob Bank terrace a few seasons back. Never knew he was a City fan but if he was there for a scrap he was a good boy to have on your side. Newport is a rough, fighting town and Newport will always raise a mob if they need to especially for Cardiff or Swansea."

Farley of NCFC explains the Newport buzz

For me, getting into football violence was always going to be a way of life. Due to my father having amber blood, it meant as kids we never missed a game, home or away. Growing up on the terraces I seen it all, from the skinheads in the late 70's to the Casuals in the early 80's battling with the likes of Pompey, Derby, Huddersfield, Cardiff, Boro and most of the teams in the old Division 3. As I started getting older, I couldn't wait for Saturdays to arrive in the hope it would kick off. By about 1986, me and my brother and a few other County Youth started to get our own little firm together and began travelling on our own. Before you know it, we had around 50-60 youth (The Youth Firm) and were having some good little 'Offs'. One of these was the time we turned up in Cardiff City Centre on a Saturday afternoon because a local rugby team from Newport was playing in the Arms Park, so this was our excuse. About 60 of us turned up outside the Owain and took a load of Cardiff by surprise. Lloydy was knocked out from behind while sipping his pint on a bar stool. Then we made our way to the Philharmonic which at the time was their main pub. By this time, word had gotten round that we were there and Cardiff were starting to mob up and head for the Philly from all directions. It went off a treat outside the Philly and was pretty much toe-to-toe for about five minutes until the Old Bill turned up. They were totally puzzled as there wasn't even a match on! A few of our lads were nicked and one did a bit of jail for going a bit mad with a bus hammer.

Cardiff used to spring surprise raids on us too. One day there was around 20 of us in John Frost Square and all of a sudden, we heard a roar go up from the flyover. We ran up there and around 30-40 Cardiff were coming towards us. After an exchange of rocks and bottles, it kicked off. We were outnumbered but gave as good as we got and stood our ground. I remember seeing Reese getting dragged from one side of the flyover to the other and the cheeky cunts robbed his jacket and trainers off him. They had stopped off on the way to or from a game which was very nice of them. For weeks after this, every time Cardiff were away we would have a good mob waiting in case they tried it on again but they never did.

However they did turn up at Maskels one Saturday night which was a Newport Skating Rink. About 30 of them came in and gave a few Newport a right kicking and did some of our lads with baseball bats. I wasn't there so I don't know exactly what happened but I heard it was quite nasty. I never really understood that one and never will. But that's Cardiff for you.

I also remember us turning up in Cardiff when they were at home to Wolves and was expecting it to be a lively day. We had planned to get to the ground just before kick-off and get into the Wolves end. We then discovered that Wolves fans had been banned from travelling so as you can imagine that we stood out a mile. We headed back to the train station but were spotted on the way in. We were heavily outnumbered so we took a bit of a kicking on the platform but it was a good day all in all.

In 1987 we played Merthyr in the Welsh Cup Final at Cardiff and turned up with 400-500 lads. I think Cardiff were expecting us but had no idea we would have such big numbers. We pretty much had our own way all day. It kicked off the minute we stepped off the train. I remember about 20 Cardiff on their toes across the bridge by the railway station. It went off again by the Philharmonic but due to our large numbers, it was all over very quickly if you know what I mean. When the Old Bill finally arrived, they escorted us to the ground and I think every pub window was smashed along the way. I think any good Cardiff boy would admit that we took them by surprise that day and we gained a lot of respect. Sadly with the demise of the former Newport County in 1989, things went downhill which for me meant following Middlesbrough and joining the 24 hour party people. Over the years I've seen some great battles between Newport and Cardiff. I'd like to say we've never got done but I will leave that shit to Swansea. County are very much still active and can still pull out a good firm but being stuck in the Blue Square South, formerly the Conference South League means we come up against very little and most of the time there is no opposition so it means relying on good cup draws and hoping we will one day get back where we belong, in the Football League. County till I die!

RIP Lem and Alan Morgan.

S of the DYC'S Story

I remember getting into football from an early age and around 15 had started getting into clobber as well. The two went hand in hand for me and soon enough there was a small group of us who wanted to emulate the older lads who we'd seen around. Our numbers were small at first and it was all new. We'd go everywhere on the train and then started hiring our own minibuses to go to away games. We had some memorable days out often culminating in lads getting lifted for this and that. Some days there would be about 16-20 of us, other times maybe just 8. After a few away days and some scrapes here and there, notably when we were fronted at New Street by an older nastier mob returning home from a game at Tamworth, we decided to give ourselves a moniker, a name to put about. It was over a few beers one evening that the Disorderly Young Casuals were born, a name that is still used loosely to this day. Lads have come and gone but the name's still about. Being young we used to cause mischief wherever we went and were lucky not to have been banned a good number of times for antics and playing up here and there. It was always hard trying to get respect from older lads but as they say, respect needs to be earned and we went about earning ours the hard way.

One Boxing Day, we had Weston-super-mare away and a car full of us went up, including some of the older lads. At half time we went into the boozer at the ground and there was a leaving committee gathered when we came to return to the ground. All told, seven of us came out and it went off with these local lads. Some say they were Bristol Rovers, some say they were Bristol City. I don't give a fuck personally and they were on top for a while as they had gas and all that caper. We managed to smash a few of them until a few more of them turned up. It ended after a good few minutes of toe-to-toes across the forecourt. It was a top day. It sparked a yearly visit down to Weston by Newport and resulted in it going off briefly a season ago on some dodgy estate. Fair play to them worzel lads, they were up for a row.

For me it was always as much if not more to do with the clobber and the general casual scene. I am absolutely infatuated with my clothes and trainers like any self respecting dresser should be and from this I've forged some very good friendships with lads from other clubs. Notably West Brom and between our younger lot and there is a healthy alliance present with West Brom lads coming with us to certain games etc.

I've always had respect for certain younger lads at Cardiff. They have always been smart and clued up on the clothes front but they do have some tossers who if given half a chance, I'm sure would like to give me a good hiding. Older lads think that because we weren't around when Newport and Cardiff were bang at it, we haven't got the hatred or an axe to grind but they're very much mistaken. We turned up on a play off final day in what I could only call one of the daftest things we ever done. Eight handed, service bus to Cardiff, got in some boozer on the edge of town and called it on.

For whatever reason, Cardiff took an age to get it together (which was probably a godsend for us) and we were nabbed by the Old Bill. I remember that we had stashed loads of bricks and wood and other stuff from a skip and were just going to give it to them as soon as they came into view. Funny enough they were halfway down the road when we were finally nabbed by plod. Other times have seen us have tit for tats with them but a good portion of them have always been sound. Things turned sour when a few Cardiff older heads jumped me and another County lad at a twang gig down the bay. A few lads I knew were there and although they weren't involved, sometimes you put two and two together and get five. That's the way it goes though. When you're a young lad coming through you really want to be at it all the time and although we've had our moments, this league isn't ideal for an aspiring lad and consequently lads lose interest. When and if we get back into the conference then I'm sure a lot of lads will come back out of the woodwork. County still get a good mob together as proved for the likes of the Jacks and Cardiff. We're there to be underestimated at your peril. These days the remaining original lads who first started the DYC thing, yours truly included, turn out with the older lot and when we have a tasty fixture which isn't very regular. The days of travelling miles and miles to follow the team is well gone but we still turn out occasionally for one off away days – notably when we went on a jolly up to Sutton where it became vicious in a boozer with a load of local pikeys and a few of ours were badly glassed. Still, as mentioned earlier, the buzz of going here, there and everywhere has been taken over by life's many vices but we're still about.

As for a younger scene over the County these days, you've a small group of lads starting out just like we did who have got into the clobber and want to make a name for themselves. Good luck to them I say. If they learn as much as I have and have stories to tell like we all have then they'll have done well.

Newport – Swansea

There's a long history between these two firms stemming from incidents in the 80's when a 17 year old Newport lad was glassed in the neck by Jacks and in revenge the Newport lads stabbed a Jack scarfer. After one game at Newport's Somerton Park in the 80's, there were 35 arrests, mostly Swansea. They were found to be carrying a variety of weapons including knives and coshes.

Newport – Swansea 2007

This game was marred by coin throwing all the way through. Fourth official Alan Sheffield copped a coin to the head which burst a blood vessel and sent him to Accident and Emergency. Newport were fined £3,000 for this and for the behaviour of Boss Alan Beadle for using abusive language in a touchline row with Mr Sheffield. Newport were also ordered to put up signs warning fans not to throw coins. Beadle was also barred from the next seven games as his behaviour had set a bad example to the already badly behaved fans.

Lemmy Bullock RIP

As already mentioned, back in the day Lemmy was Newport's main boy. He was game as fuck and wouldn't run from anyone. He took some shocking hidings over the years (and dished out some) but still kept coming back for more. He used to lead the raiding parties into Cardiff and was hated but also respected by Cardiff's main boys. His life came to a tragic end as he was murdered by drug dealers in Harvey's pub in Pill, Newport. Word has it that he had argued with the dealers because he didn't like them selling that shit in his town. They had threatened him and Lemmy being Lemmy wouldn't back down so three of them jumped him. He died from serious stab wounds to the stomach. His three attackers, Mohammed Nasser, Aaron Kent and Martyn Bruce were banged up for a total of 60 years but that's no good to Lemmy's kids.

The Bognor Game

In 2006 the Newport County boys all turned out for a game against Bognor in tribute to Lemmy. A mixture of the grief and anger over his death mixed with alcohol meant the game turned into a mini riot. A brawl erupted in the clubhouse which was wrecked and fans battled with police who had to release dogs to restore order. Lemmy's mother slammed the behaviour and said she understood how they felt but that they should have kept it dignified. I bet if Lemmy could have seen it though, he would have been smiling to himself. RIP a top boy from the old school.

Docksider explains the score with County.

"Well how do you explain a non-league team turning out 300+ lads? And I do mean serious lads. I'll try to explain why the best I can. When Newport County folded back in the late 80's, they had a nasty little mob loosely known as the 'B' team who were stuck with the major problem of life in the doldrums of non-league football. I mean right at the bottom as the side was resurrected but had to go the same route as any other new side. For those of you that have been there, you will know it's not a pretty site or place to be. They didn't even have a ground in Newport so they had to play their home games in a little town/village in England in front of crowds of a few hundred at the most. So what were the options for the mob they had? Go watch their team with no chance whatsoever of any action? Pack it in all together and hope to god they climb the league ladder as soon as possible? Go to another club and ply their trades there? The latter is easier said than done as your closest teams are your bitterest rivals so you're hardly going to be welcomed with open arms. Or you go further afield and do your best to get accepted. So the mob divided into these three options and stayed active best they could. So you see the mob never really went away. In fact it grew and became more vicious as the clubs that were chosen were chosen for their firms not their team's positions in the league. So now when Newport who thankfully play back in their home town, have a game that looks like it has a possibility for trouble these lads return in their numbers. Throw into that that every lunatic from the town will turn out as well because they know everyone else will be there. Don't forget that this doesn't happen every week as they're still non-league and only a handful of games have possibilities. But you can be assured that when these games arise, there's a mob that has to be seen to be believed. I've sat in boozers next to very well known lads from other firms who've seen it all and bought the T-shirts and overheard them on their mobiles saying, "Fuck me, you wanna see this," when they've came for a day out with Newport.

It's just a mass of men, mainly over 30 who turn out for the chance of a bit of action and the love of their first team, Newport County. Many have came and many have tried and many have had the privilege of getting a visit. For sure, many will continue to do so.

COUNTY 'TIL WE DIE!

Cardiff v Newport 2008

These days, Newport County can still raise a good few hundred boys as they showed last week when they brought 400 boys to Ninian Park. Cardiff were expected to have at least that many boys to confront them. This was rumoured to become the biggest tear up between the two old rivals since the 80's and adding spice to the menu was the fact that 15 Newport had been beaten up by a much larger gang of Cardiff in Milan and one Newport fan was slashed. In the event, Cardiff had NOBODY about and at most, 40 boys were around with many of them being Under 5's (Youngsters).

Docksider of Newport gives his view of the nights events:
"I cannot believe that after all the 'lets hope they show this time' crap from the Cardiff contingent on this site that it was you lot that didn't show - at your own ground as well. We had 200+ lads today who had all made the effort after being told you were right up for it. We sent our youth down first to check the water and they were straight into what Cardiff there was waiting for them. One of yours was hit by a motor in the melee, hope he's ok. We arranged for taxis, vans, etc as we were told to do by you again. Only four taxis and a transit managed to get through because yet another accident stopped any traffic for at least an hour. Those that were unlucky enough to get down there were unopposed in every boozer they went in and the Old Bill still none the wiser. Another 50 who had gone down on an earlier bus, were wrapped up by your Old Bill straight away and put in another of your empty boozers. Our main mob was easy 150+ lads plus another 100 scarfers had no option but to go with the main escort on the train.

We were expecting/hoping to be attacked on the way to the ground but it only happened 3-4 times. Every time we broke the escort and had to chase the little mobs that did decide to have a go. A few arrests there but that happens and I think all the 200 were prepared to get arrested on the night. We were in constant contact with the Cardiff that did make the effort all night but they said straight that they only had 40 up for it. We were asked to try to leave early as it would be the last chance of any dancing. The Old Bill were hoping to keep us in for a while but as soon as we knew our hosts were outside we steamed what Old Bill were in the ground. A few more attempted arrests I think but we breezed past them and got outside. Never seen us so efficient and violent and a five minute battle with your baton happy police was the highlight of our day after spanking you on the pitch of course. At one time they actually fled themselves due to our numbers but releasing their dogs and horse cops forced us on the back foot for the first time all day.

Then fuck did they steam into us and unfortunately fists and boots are no match for the by now almost equal numbers of the psychotic Nazi police in full attire. How we had no serious casualties is amazing because a few of ours were out cold. All we could do to save them was to drag them with us as we received wave after wave of the bastards who were by now loving the free for all. The scene on the train was like a hospital ward but the only complaint was your lack of effort, organisation and bottle on the day.

Even our own police thought they'd have a go on our arrival but were brushed aside. They are a joke compared to the loons you have down there. Please don't say you've bigger fish to fry, it was too cold or you weren't allowed out because you knew we were coming and either bottled it or thought the mob you had out would have been enough. But they were far from that, they were.

Full respect to your lads that did try to sort out something. Maybe bullshit as you can't believe the Old Bill at the best of times but it was nice to hear we were as good as anything they've come up against. For a shitty little non-league side either we are pretty good or others have given you too much respect. Will be nice to see the replies to this from those that did bother to turn out as they must be somewhat peeved themselves at your lack of effort."

'BC' of the Soul Crew Replies:

"We were utter wank. After weeks and weeks of every cunt saying, "Yeah, I'll be at so and so pub and so and so time," we get a shitty 50-60. Twenty of us met early doors down Cathedral Road and were almost instantly found by the Old Bill. As they radio for backup, we all split up and get into cars and taxis. We then mob up at The Claude in Roath. We get a good 30-40 in there before the Old Bill yet again show up. A few of us kick through the fire exit and fuck off, hoping the rest would follow. Did they fuck. Four of us left! Climbed into a car and had a look around. Word was that Newport were at the Royal Oak so we go and have a look. Low and behold as we pass, there's 30-40 Newport in there with no Old Bill. We go back to The Claude and get a few lads to jump over the back wall. 10, yes 10, of us walked down to the Royal Oak on a suicide mission only for one of our lads to get run over on the way. That put me out of action for about an hour because I wanted to know if the lad was alright. By the time I arrived at Grangetown, there was a mob of younger Cardiff running around attacking escorts and all that bollocks.

No excuses here. We were shit yesterday. Don't think many people realised you were coming in force. I kept telling people, "They had 200 for Swansea last season so they'll bring that here," but no one listened. Ah well, hats off to Newport.

Full respect from me to Newport, one of the most organised firms in Wales it seems at the moment. They only turn out two or three times a season but when they do, they have a right nasty bunch who would take some shifting."

AA gives his opinion of the nights events and of Newport

"NEWPORT. Fair play to them on that night. Newport were by far better than us. All we had was 30 lads in Grangetown after the game and 20 max in the car park. But this was Newport's CUP FINAL. To the average City lad, they don't even rate Newport and wouldn't even bother to think about turning up for them. In the 80's, it was Cardiff's local Trendies v Newport not Cardiff's main firm. Week in week out, it was Cardiff Trendies and about 30 Barry Trendies who would battle in the nights with Newport. Some weeks we would muster up 30 lads. Other weeks up to 70 of us would go to Newport and fair play to them, they would always oblige us. Many times we run them ragged but we also came unstuck on a few occasions. On about three surprise visits to Cardiff by them, they done the business but I remember when they attacked Brownhill's that they didn't half take a pasting from us then by Viking and Co. Going back to the Welsh Invitation Cup in 2008, I would say Newport brought a well game mob of anything up to 180 OLD SCHOOL LADS and they would of given any league club a run for their money and perhaps done most. The problem is our Valleys' mobs DON'T RATE them so unless it's a game that means anything, they will never turn up for them. In Milan, they fought an awesome battle with a group of our Docks lads and Newport were smashed. I will never forget what Viking and Jonathan said to me. "Newport were game as fuck but in the end we fucked them and we did it for you for what they did at their place. 40 onto 1 and even then they attacked you from behind when you were with a woman." Jonathan said, "That was the night we lost respect for Newport."

I have a lot of memories of Newport and they were fun days. To this day I still have great respect for a lad called 'Adams' who was game as fuck and never ran. But we all move on and those were the 80's. Sorry County, the lads who were with me in the 80's have mostly all moved on. If we drew you in the FA Cup, I'm sure Cardiff will oblige you and you'll need your 180 lads then. Those days in the 80's will always be there to remember but you lost my respect with the 40 onto 1 in the year 2000."

In the aftermath of this game against Cardiff and after the police attacked the Newport lads outside the ground horrifically injuring a few of them, they launched the predictable witch-hunt in the papers with photos and a number to grass up those they wanted to arrest. 36 arrests followed and at the time of writing, they are all facing court on public order charges. The CPS is applying for football banning orders for all of them. Looks like the powers that be have earmarked Newport's firm to be the next one they smash up as they've done successfully all over the country.

Violence planned? Thugs may have tuned into police radio

RUNNING BATTLES... A reporter-officer comes to make a series on scene but strike is forced on throw at the flashpoint in Cardiff's city centre last Saturday

SOCCER YOBS ON RAMPAGE

By Gareth Phillips and Sam Black

VIOLENCE flared last night as the pre-season matches between Cardiff City and Swindon Town exploded into scenes of unrest.

Police blocked off the road and the balconies had been closed making it a group of about 30 fans walking up and...

Fans clash in city centre pub

Brawling: Chaos as fights spill into street

By Argus reporter

FIGHTING football fans caused chaos in Newport and forced the closure of a busy city centre pub.

Brawling broke out just before 7pm on Saturday when a group of Cardiff supporters – returning from their club's match against Swindon Town – clashed with Newport County fans in the Wetherspoons pub on Cambrian Road.

Chairs were thrown and glasses smashed inside the pub and customers fled the pub as the large punch-up spilled onto the street where axes and knives were fighting.

But they wanted before police arrived and some witnesses believe the skirmish was pre-meditated.

Mal Lamrani, the manager of Lloyd's pub, near Wetherspoons, said: "I was driving to work in the morning and I could tell some-

thing was happening because there was all these new faces in Newport. There was quite a lot of skinheads all dressed smartly standing at different points in the city centre.

"There was a really bad atmosphere – you just knew something was brewing. Then all of a sudden, a group of about six or seven men ran up Cambrian Road from outside The Lamb public house and barged into Wetherspoons.

"There were occasions reaching out of the pub as the fighting was going on. It looked a pre-meditated plan to include local boys and they sang back on the train.

"It was almost as if they knew the police organised to establish the police and throw quickly."

A spokesman for Wetherspoons, which had to close for around 15 minutes following the incident, confirmed

there had been an incident on Saturday evening but could not comment further.

Inspector Steve Payton, of Gwent police, said: "There was an altercation between Newport and Cardiff fans on Saturday evening. There were two serious injuries at the pub and two occasions of minor cuts and bruises.

"We had around 30 people exchanging blows and chairs were also thrown but by the time police arrived the fighting had dispersed. The city centre and the police do not welcome this type of activity. It will not be tolerated and it will be policed accordingly."

The clash was the latest in a long line of battles between the two clubs. Two years ago, Cardiff and Newport fans clashed outside Newport Stadium following a pre-season friendly between the two teams. The more recent brawl led to eight arrests.

● Editorial comment: page 12

Two held: Newport men blamed for match brawls

SOCCER FANS IN PUB FIGHTS

By Paul Platt

Our cameraman attacked by mob

AN ARGUS photographer became the target of a baying mob of "supporters" at the match.

The photographer, who is not being named, was punched during a "terrifying" ten minutes during the first half of the Newport County v Cardiff tie.

Around 30 fans turned on him as he tried to take pictures of a brawl in the car park beside the gantry inside the ground.

He said: "My view was of up to 30 fans shouting abuse and gesturing against the perimeter fence trying to get out onto the car park.

"They pushed through to get closer to the fight and police were quick to intercept.

"They immediately turned and tried to get back into the ground.

"I stopped taking pictures,

... realised I had become the target of their aggression."

As the fans inside turned ... back to the match as police broke up the fighting outside, they turned on the Argus photographer who had been standing on a gantry inside the ground.

He added: "They started demanding my camera and film and someone threw a punch which hit me on the top of the head.

"There were punches being thrown and I was being pushed.

"It went on for long enough for all the possibilities to go through my mind. It was terrifying.

"The crowd was of all ages and they seemed intent on aggression.

"I was just trying to keep on my feet and keep hold of the camera.

"I think I was lucky to come out of it with nothing more than a broken mobile phone.

"I got back inside the perimeter fence on the pitch and they did not follow. I must have had a guardian angel."

FLARE-UP: Newport and Cardiff fans clash

Chapter Seven
Wrexham's Frontline

In North Wales is Wrexham with its long established firm, 'The Frontline'. They have been very active over the years and are much more likely to travel to Wales games than the Jacks. My personal experience of Wrexham is that every time we have met, we have battered them and one time we even ran them at their own ground but I've been told by a lot of people that they have a game little firm and have had their moments. Cardiff boys have had some memorable scraps with them over the years at Wales games at home and abroad. A mate of mine who follows Liverpool said they were attacked by Wrexham at a pre-season friendly last year - he said the Scousers shit themselves.

I don't know what it is with North Wales police but maybe they haven't a lot else to do as they seem to have carried out a lot of targeting operations on Wrexham over the years; a lot more than most forces and I suspect this has hit their ability to perform. I know one of their main boys 'Neil' had to step down after constant police harassment. The CPS in the area have announced that they are getting tough on hooligans. Chief Prosecutor for the area, Ed Pepperami, said, "We are going to show hooligans the red card. Hooligans hate and fear banning orders so we will use them as a key weapon against them." The North Wales Chief Police Inspector said, "There are currently 51 banning orders in place against so-called Wrexham supporters. The genuine supporter does not want to be subjected to racism, obscene language or physical attack."

Racism? What do they mean? Wrexham aren't racist are they? Well maybe some are as anti-Polish graffiti has been sprayed all around the area and their main enemies are Shrewsbury's 'English Border Front' (where I once took a kicking) and Chester's 125's firm. Anti-English chanting is an essential part of playing any English team as is their abuse of us so maybe that's what they mean? Then there's the Caia Park riots which police claim was orchestrated by some senior Frontline members.

The Caia Park riots occurred on the Caia Park Estate in Wrexham, Wales on 22nd June 2003 and involved violence between Iraqi Kurds, local residents and police. The violence began when Hoshank Baker Kader (an Iraqi) was set upon by local residents. Approximately 20 of the Kurdish immigrants in response armed themselves and attacked the Red Dragon pub at about 8:05pm believing that the perpetrators of violence to their compatriot were inside. The drinkers inside returned the violence using bar stools and snooker cue sticks. From then on the riot spread with local residents taking an active response and attempting to get to the Kurdish area of the estate. Police were called by the landlord of the pub and proceeded to round up troublemakers.

The riots against the police happened the following night when a variety of missiles including petrol bombs, stones and bottles were thrown by a crowd of angry locals. At the height of the incident, a crowd of approximately 200 youths attacked about 25 police officers. This assault lasted for three hours. The police discovered to their cost that several factors prevented them from quelling the disorder quickly. Senior officers underestimated the potential for disorder following the initial night and only drafted in a small number of extra officers from Wrexham county and Flintshire. None of these officers were initially deployed in riot equipment and were unprepared for the rapid escalation in aggression from local people. When rioting began it proved difficult to summon extra resources to the scene due to a number of issues. The remoteness of the western area of the North Wales force meant that rapid support was summoned from three neighbouring forces in England. These were Cheshire, Merseyside and West Mercia. Despite their image as a rural force, it was only officers from parts of West Mercia who arrived in time to provide assistance. Many of these officers travelled from as far afield as Hereford. The vehicles used by Wrexham Police were also found to be ill-equipped for disorder and a significant amount of damage occurred to them. Despite these problems and despite several injuries sustained by those deployed, the officers on the ground acquitted themselves well and received widespread praise.

During subsequent nights, riot police from North Wales and Merseyside maintained a heavy presence in the town to prevent further disorder and to arrest the main participants. This approach led to a great deal of criticism from people in Caia Park who felt that they were all being punished for the behaviour of many people from outside the estate. The violence shocked many in the local area and attracted attention throughout the UK and perhaps not surprisingly, support from the BNP. Fortunately there were no fatalities related to the events of 22nd June but injuries were suffered by police officers and some Kurds. At the trial at Mold Crown Court, 51 people were sentenced in relation to the riots with a combined time between them of 80 years in prison. The youngest perpetrator was only 13 years old and was sentenced to 4 years in a secure unit. Major changes occurred in the area as a result of the troubles. The Kurdish/Iraqi population were subsequently distributed throughout the county to smaller communities. The police were given extra funding by the Home Office to increase Community officers on the estate.

That's what happens when you dump a load of asylum seekers in a rough place like this and allow them to walk around in gangs, allegedly drug dealing and intimidating people. The Welsh people won't have it. Simple as that. Blaming football hooligans for social problems like this is bollocks and an easy way out for those looking for excuses. In Cardiff in the early 90's, you had the 'Ely Bread riots' which was blamed on racism and on football hooligans just because it all started when an Asian shopkeeper locked up a kid that he had caught stealing in his shop and he was in dispute with another shop over the right to sell bread. The media jumping all over it and calling it 'racist' and saying it was orchestrated by football hooligans which no doubt sentenced the people unfortunate enough to be arrested a lot longer in jail.

Wrexham – Chester

To the Frontline, games against Chester are the equivalent of the Cardiff-Swansea derbies. The hatred runs deep. There have been many well documented clashes between the two and the police class this as a high risk fixture.

Police arrest 34 in street fights

By DAVID HOLMES

FOOTBALL hooligans run amok as Chester City fans clashed with local rivals Wrexham before the crucial FA cup tie.

Police made a total of 34 arrests, including 12 for affray, after fans rampaged down Watergate Street on Friday.

Two others were locked up for assaults on police - although no officers were seriously injured.

The remainder were arrested for public order offences.

One witness, who got caught up in the main trouble in the city centre at about 4.45pm, before the match, said there were about 30 Chester fans and about 30 Wrexham fans involved in an incident.

"The Wrexham fans were chanting and then they chased the Chester fans down the street," he said.

"I hid in the Rows - it was quite frightening. All the pubs locked their doors."

Sgt Keith Sutton, of Chester police, said there had been several isolated incidents before, during and after the game.

He disclosed that many Wrexham fans had been dropped off in Handbridge and made their way into town via the Groves.

At one stage police had been aware of a group of 200 supporters walking along Pepper Street and up Bridge Street.

The group split up into smaller groups with some going down Watergate Street and others making their way up Northgate Street and down past the Princess Street bus exchange.

"It was a case of the match being spoilt by the minority," he said.

"It is always the minority that cause the problems - the majority of groups were OK."

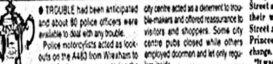

Four-page FA Cup special – see full-colour centre spread

● TROUBLE had been anticipated and about 80 police officers were available to deal with any trouble.

Police motorcyclists acted as lookouts on the A483 from Wrexham to watch for large groups entering the city.

Extra patrols were laid on at Handbridge, where many Wrexham fans arrived during the afternoon before going drinking in the city centre. High-profile police foot patrols in the city centre acted as a deterrent to trouble-makers and offered reassurance to visitors and shoppers. Some city centre pubs closed while others employed doormen and let only regulars inside.

Barrie Hipkiss, chairman of Chester City FC Supporters Club said "It's sad in this day and age. It's the same at every local derby. The rivalry between fans seems to be something we have got to live with at the moment."

Chester away, 2004, LDV

"This game had been built up ever since the draw was made. It was the first time that we had played them for 7 years and for most of the young lads', it was their first trip to Chester. The youth had already arranged a minibus and ended up meeting the older lads in town and all going together. Older lads had been on the phone to Chester all day with Chester claiming to have 50+ but wouldn't tell us where they were. We decided the best bet would be Handbridge so we ended up in The White Horse with about 60 lads.

RAMPAGE IN THE STREETS

City fans' violent clash was arranged on mobile phones

By NATALIE BARNETT

MORE than 50 rival football fans armed with pool cues went on the rampage through Chester streets and pubs in a vicious, organised mass brawl.

Police say the clash involved Chester and Wrexham football fans who travelled in to the city by train after attending their teams' away matches.

Police flooded into the city just after 8pm after reports that the fans had smashed every window in the Deva Mail Sports and Social club in City Road. Police say fans used mobile phones to arrange the punch-up which left many people unconscious and needing hospital treatment.

The brawl continued through the streets of Chester bringing traffic to a standstill as fans use pool cues to smash the windows of parked cars.

Police have made three arrests but there is more to follow. Detectives are scanning CCTV footage in a bid to snare the offenders.

Warned

Chester Chief Inspector Dave Hill said police were in vigorous pursuit of those involved and warned that violent crime of this nature would not be tolerated.

A police statement said: "Chester and Wrexham fans travelled by train into Chester on Saturday. The fans went into a licensed premises in City Road at 8.15pm. There the fans bumped into each other and violent disorder followed."

Anyone with any information should contacts the police on 01244 350222.

news@chestereveningleader.co.uk

■ Smashed windows at the Deva Mail club in City Road after trouble flared between Chester and Wrexham fans in the city on Saturday.

More lads arrived as time went on, giving us a mob of about 120 altogether with a decent youth showing of about 30. We found out that Chester had been locked in a pub in Blacon with no chance of getting out so a lot of lads took out their frustrations on the Old Bill. Missiles were thrown including stools, tables and pool balls and windows were smashed as well as the fire alarm being set off. Eventually we were rounded up and put on a bus to the ground. We didn't see any Chester on the way and the bus was smashed up, resulting in us having to walk back after the game.

The game passed without much incident except for a bit of trouble with a few Wrexham in the home end but nowt major. After the game, about 10 Wrexham older lads broke away from the escort and ended up having it with 20 tooled up Chester shithouses. Wrexham eventually managed to get on top mainly due to the fact that the Chester decided to drop their weapons. We had a military style escort back to the station and again, we didn't see any Chester around. All in all, Chester were disappointing but the Old Bill made it nearly a complete non event. Still, the result almost made up for that!"

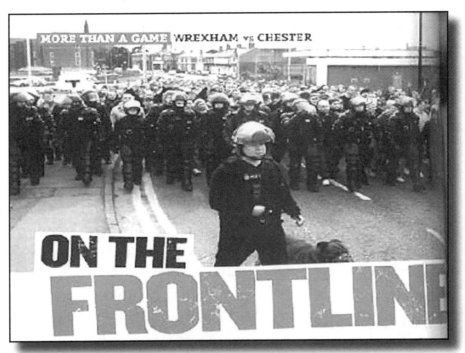

Version of Brentford Away from D of the Wrexham Youth

"Many stories have been told about this encounter but this is a first hand account which will state some home truths. Brentford by the looks of it will never agree with it. The facts are that 3 Wrexham Youth were attacked by 15-20 Brentford Youth. No Brentford Youth were seen in the game and for that matter, no Brentford older lads - no Brentford, full stop. Apparently we had been giving it the big one to them all game? Not quite sure how as they must have been on the terrace behind the goal. Like I said, we couldn't see any Brentford lads in the ground. So it's a bit of a shock when 3 of you get fronted at full time outside. Anyway, we let it be known that we think it a bit silly fronting 3 lads when there 15 odd handed. Still they carried on with their bullying session. Only thing was the 3 Wrexham lads weren't melting. After walking a good 300 yards surrounded by Brentford Youth, the Brentford Youth couldn't resist and had their best go at giving it to the 3 Wrexham. That's the facts. The Wrexham were saved from getting a real good beating by the Old Bill. Brentford were on their toes once the Old Bill showed. Funny thing was one of the Brentford lads still walked off with claret on his fake Stone Island jumper due to the Wrexham giving it their best shot. Brentford also took it upon themselves to rob one of the Wrexham lads of his cap. Yes, very big, I know."

Operation Advance

Police raided homes across North Wales, the Wirral and Cheshire following a 5 month investigation into clashes on a train at Rock Ferry and in Chester City Centre. Officers arrested 36 hooligans as part of 'Operation Advance'. All were charged with conspiracy to cause violent disorder. Merseyside police knew of the plan to meet at the Prince William pub for a battle after intercepting text messages between the conspirators including one which read 'Wrexham, they're bringing 200 or more, can't wait'. At trial, 32 fans were sentenced to a total of 31½ years in prison. The judge said, "Tranmere Rovers has always enjoyed the highest respect and reputation in the football world." Yeh, right-oh mate! Tranmere's always been known as a horrible shithole where getting slashed up if caught on your own or in small groups is a very likely prospect. Many times our boys have been chased with blades at Tranmere and one time Jerky and a few others had to run off down the railway tracks to avoid being carved up. The guys chasing them turned their attention to a lone Liverpool scarfer on the platform and gave him over 200 stitches - the fucking animals.

Wrexham – Swansea 2002

Police in riot gear were drafted in as rival fans clashed in Wrexham town centre. Two people were arrested during the clashes and police are expecting to make further arrests in connection with the incidents. The police helicopter was drafted in as fans battled in the town centre and the Turf pub. A trail of damage was left at various pubs and one policeman was injured after being hit with a bottle.

Wrexham v Port Vale 2004

A children's football coach from Stoke was amongst a dozen soccer hooligans who were jailed after Wrexham's 2-1 win at the Racecourse. The court was told that the rival thugs had dodged police and ran through peoples' gardens fighting and pelting each other with bricks and garden gnomes. One Wrexham fan, Mark Williams was jailed for 9 months as he was already the subject of a banning order.

Wrexham Lad's recollection of Belgium

"70 of us travelled there on a double decker bus which took two days to get to Brussels. As we stepped off the bus and made our way to the hotel, the Cardiff Docks lot suddenly all steamed into us from nowhere. It kicked off big time for ages until the Old Bill turned up and separated us with tear gas. We were held in custody for three days then deported. It was mental. After that, the Cardiff lads gave us loads of respect and there hasn't really been any bother between us since. We have teamed up a few times at Wales games."

Cardiff Lad says:

"Wrexham used to get it in the neck quite a bit. They were going to Wales games knowing full well that Cardiff ran the show. There was loads of hostility. They had to fight their corner a good few times but fuck all would stop them following their country. That's why they are respected by the Cardiff lot. Some good friendships have been formed over the years between us based on mutual respect. Swansea which is twice the size of Wrexham, don't have the same bottle. It's as simple as that."

My conclusion on Wrexham is that you can see they have a good little firm. Although they don't match up to the bigger firms, they can still be a dangerous bunch and have shown themselves to be still flying the flag at every opportunity. They recently attacked a pub full of Scousers at a pre-season friendly which you can't fault them for. A good bunch of lads who deserve some respect.

Football violence filmed

A video recording of the brawl involving dozens of rival fans at an amateur football match has been offered to the police.

The recording, made by a Saughall team supporter, is believed to show the faces of hooligans who broke up the Wrexham Lager Amateur Cup semi-final at Gresford at the weekend.

A Chester man suffered a broken leg when violence broke out at the game between the Cambrian Vaults, Wrexham, and the Saughall Vernon Institute.

Saughall club chair-

man, Mr Peter Bond, confirmed today that police had been offered the video recording in an effort to catch the hooligans.

"We usually make recordings of important matches to play back to players after the game", hes aid:

North East Wales Football Association secretary Mr Keith Spencer said today that arrangements were being made to replay the semi-final at a safer venue.

Mr Bond has called for the match re-play to be in the morning before the pubs open.

Chester fan cops a broken leg (there's a shame)

POLICE were called to break-up a running battle between Wrexham and Oldham Athletic fans that left a man in hospital and a trail of devastation in its wake.

ences were ripped up for weapons, gardens damaged and a bus window smashed in the brawl, which resulted in two people needing medical treatment.

One Wrexham man is in a 'stable' condition in the Maelor Hospital today after he was glassed in the incident.

The violence began half an hour before kick-off, marring the Reds eventual 3-1 win over their promotion rivals.

Scores of police were called to Chester Road amid scenes of violence likened to the scenes of hooliganism from the 1980s.

The incident happened as Oldham fans drinking in the Four Dogs pub were spotted by a number of Wrexham fans travelling past on a bus.

Two fans injured in running battle

The away supporters ran after the vehicle smashing its rear window and forcing the fans off the bus, starting the fight.

Eyewitness Haydn Taylor said: "The scenes and running battles were amazing and terrifying and the police's reaction seemed very slow.

Weapon

"Fights were everywhere and fans were ripping pieces of wooden fences from gardens in an attempt to make a weapon they could use."

The Four Dogs' landlady, Celia Warburton, confirmed that Oldham fans were drinking in the pub.

She said: "Most were outside but when they saw the bus go past some of

them raced after it. The next thing we knew the police were here."

Wrexham Police received 22 emergency 999 calls from worried residents during the incident.

They managed to stop the fighting and the police helicopter was launched to track fleeing troublemakers.

Sgt Andrew Davies, of North Wales Police's eastern control room, said they had made no arrests following the incident.

"We managed to separate the fans and usher them towards the ground," he said.

"The helicopter was launched as a precaution to keep an eye on the situation so we could act quickly if another incident arose."

Chapter Eight
Cardiff in the 70's

A Mancs version of his trip to Cardiff in the 70's

"I remember arriving from Paddington (see we had plenty of cockney followers in those crap Div 2 days.) I was just a schoolboy and although I'd been to plenty of games at Old Trafford with my old fella, I'd only been to a few tame aways at the time. The Cardiff game was unlike anything I think I have ever seen before or since. We expected an 'interesting' day to say the least but nothing prepared two spotty kids for an afternoon of absolute mayhem the likes of which, (I'm sure anyone who was there will heartily agree) has never been seen since with perhaps the exception of Luton v Millwall or other such ground-breaking occasions.

United fans were largely untouchable in those days. Sheer weight of numbers plus a ferocious bravado that wouldn't allow them to back down from any resistance. Even the southern counterparts, Chelsea, West Ham and to some extent Millwall were still lagging behind in both exploits and organization. So it was with that air of self confidence that we alighted the station. "Manchester la la la" rang out all around as we sauntered and swaggered our way towards Ninian Park, our summer holiday homework problems left aside as we strutted our stuff with the big boys, the exhilaration of being surrounded by 100 or so 'grown men' of 18!

There we spotted a group of about 100 lads. A cheer went up. These were more of our own we assumed. To this day, I'll never forget the scene. A handful of our 'comrades' from across the road ambled over, a reuniting embrace was no doubt to follow as these old friends joined the throng. Suddenly I noticed the crazed grin on the face of the approaching stranger and even with my limited knowledge of football away trips, I had a feeling all was not well. Our mate with the mental mug simply smashed his fist into the face of one of our lads. "Bloody hell, they're Cardiff bastards," came the cry. The lone assailant then began wading in to at least 10 of the United group, bodies were going down all around. His 99 or so mates did very little to assist this lone kamikaze mission. Either they were terrified of the situation or maybe knew his capabilities. Maybe this was Frank the Legend from the newspaper stories?

Finally, the two groups snapped out of their frozen apathy and charged into each other with a manic relish. Now when people say 200 fans were fighting 'toe-to-toe' they usually mean half a dozen at most with the rest milling about looking stupid but this was as it sounded with scenes reminiscent of a gargantuan scale WWF tag match. My friend and I stood there dumbstruck. It was over 25 years ago and I would love to have been able to recall how I joined in the scene of carnage, downing all-comers but as a young boy, I was horror-stricken and frozen with terror. I remember one Policeman ambling by and peering round the corner to see what all the noise was. He took one look at the scene and carried on walking. Classic!

By this time most of our group had been split into small factions and the walk to the ground was quite simply a journey into some apocalyptic nightmare. It was as if my mate and I had just emerged from the Tardis into some post-nuclear wasteland. Yet there was no Jon Pertwee to close those bloody Police-Box doors and I guess most of the Coppers would have been in there hiding if they could have! On every street corner, the sights were the same. People scurrying around in all directions. I saw one outlandish figure. It was United fan in a white boiler-suit and black bowler hat giving out instructions looking like an extra from 'A Clockwork Orange'. All around were cries of 'here they are', 'don't run', 'I've got one'. A whirl of confusion, a tidal wave of thundering red Doctor Marten boots and tartan scarves.

We arrived outside the ground and met up again with some faces from the train. Some looked dazed and confused, others bloodied but belligerent. "See this," said one half-caste Londoner with a bloody nose, "the next Taffy I see, I'm going to give him three of these." We all laughed loudly at the ridiculous statement, though from some of the characters I had seen at the Station encounter, a guy with three noses was highly likely.

With about an hour to go before kick-off, we decided to opt for some sustenance to re-fuel our adrenaline loss. A pink, undercooked 'Spam burger' did the trick for 30p. We started queuing at the rather oddly named 'Bob Bank' whatever that was. Suddenly a group of Reds walked past us, full of contempt that we were planning to go into our own end. "Not in here you arseholes, it's all down 'The Grange'." Intimidated by their ridicule, we followed our heroes and paid in at the 'Grange'. As we prepared to pay our 70p, I noticed some of the lads around us were tying their scarves around their waists out of sight. I now realised that occupying the home end was more of a military operation than a consumer choice. We gathered 'inconspicuously' at a point close to the fence which had a huge no-man's land separating the rival fans. Insults were traded for half an hour. A few blood curdling screams of bravado followed by a couple of half-hearted charges by either side at the fence. A fat Cardiff fan with a scarf round his wrist and tomato sauce stains around his chin, shouted something indistinguishable and launched a wooden stake, like a mini telegraph pole into the baying United mob.

A few cheers rang out as it hit an unseen target. Instantly a piece of concrete was hurled into the Cardiff boys to my right and I could see a small group of people huddled round a fallen comrade. The reality that someone really could die here today (possibly even me) hit home and I wondered how my parent's would react if they knew that I wasn't actually on the 'day trip to Barry Island' that I was supposed to be on with my mate's 'caring Dad'.

As if it wasn't bad enough, things were about to take a turn for the worse. A small group of Bluebirds began to take an unhealthy interest in the dozen or so lads to their left (us). One hideous freak with a severely scarred face wandered over. "Not singing boys? We all sing in here, you're all a bit quiet today. You are all 'Care-diff' I hope." My heart sank. Rumbled and we knew they weren't going to go away now their suspicions were aroused. The scout ambled back to the main group to report his findings. After a brief chin-wag amongst themselves, three or four more came over for an 'interview'. The 'Head of Personnel' was none other than the fearsome one-man war machine we had seen in action near the station. I wanted to cry and explain that I had a note from my Mum that said on no account was I to have my head kicked in as I had a cold. I guess that a rat, when cornered, will strike out and I found that I was surrounded by a few heavy-duty rodents. "You want a song do you?" piped up a ginger-haired Northerner. "Yooooh-niiiiii-ted," he bellowed in a slow ponderous scream like Hitler addressing the Nuremberg Rally. That was the signal for all out attack. The dozen or so infiltrators charged upwards at the massed ranks of blue-scarved savages in a suicidal attack. Fists flew and a sea parted between the fans as the visitors gained some amazing ground. I cowered behind a mouth-foaming long-haired Red with the most enormous baggy trousers I have ever seen, confidant that they wouldn't see me behind the expanse of bottle green material. The very trousers that must have inspired Suggs' Madness hit some years later.

Suddenly the 'Red Sea' in front of me became just a pond as the Cardiff boys attacked the small numbers involved in the kamikaze charge. Then it dried up like a Midsummer's day in the Serengeti as the United boys were now charging back down the same stairs that they had scaled so heroically a few moments earlier. I just wanted the concrete to open up and swallow me, yet most of the concrete in Ninian Park was of the airborne variety. It was now clear that we were in serious trouble and we seized the chance to make for a gap in the faltering fencing, weakened by numerous charges. We raced towards the safety of our fellow fans who, to our horror, on seeing the onrushing mob charged into us and a number of fists flew before our identity was established.

We were then welcomed like a band of soldiers returning from a daring mission behind enemy lines which I guess it had been. I was terrified as huge lumps of brick, concrete and wood were flying over from both sides. The Police were desperately trying to contain the two fearsome mobs who charged continually at the horror-stricken thin blue line and at several points it looked as though the fence would give way.

As a veteran of away trips at home and abroad throughout the 70's, 80's and to a lesser extent the 21st century, I can honestly say I couldn't imagine the carnage that would have taken place had that wilting police line given way on that day. Mercifully it held and despite sickening chants of 'Munich' and occasionally even 'Aberfan' and about enough flying ballast to build a high-rise block, the body count was surprisingly low. People were being carried out from both sides on stretchers, many with horrifying head wounds, struggling yobs were being plucked from both ranks by those Policemen plucky enough to try. Others were met with a volley of missiles and feet. Every so often a small group of United fans would emerge in the home section and the same scenario would be played out – a suicidal charge followed by submersion beneath a frenzy of kicks, stamps and punches.

By now, I had retreated to the safety of a piece of grass next to the stinking cesspit that passed for the 'Gentleman's Toilets'. Still numb with the day's events and relieved to know I definitely wasn't dead, I rested against a small wall. A small group of boys made their way past, having just come through the turnstiles. Latecomers, they've missed all the action, I thought. Suddenly I recognised one of the faces. Missed the action? They were the action! That same horrible mush, that messed-up mug. It was our old friend the Welsh war-machine. He was now amongst us! Totally unnoticed he made his way to the top of the stairs. I wanted to scream, to yell pantomime style, "he's behind you!" but to no avail.

Without even a glance to ensure his six mates were in tow, he just proceeded to steam into all and sundry, a whirling, devastating threshing machine that took about a dozen boys to suppress. Even then he seemed to be unscathed, just made his point and then made a sensible but dignified retreat. To this day I wonder who he was and just what kind of legend he was around Grangetown or the like. The match was played out in a kind of surreal haze and on the final whistle, both sides burst from the terraces into the street where ingenious Police plans ensured the two armies took separate routes home and were kept apart for all of two minutes.

Just as before, during the game, it had seemed that I had an awful knack of arriving just as major disorder was breaking out. So it was to be the pattern on the journey back to the station. Sporadic bottles and missiles flew but no major incidents occurred until the station was in sight. Suddenly this was to be the major convergence of both main mobs and hundreds of Cardiff and Manchester boys tore into each other. There was none of this puffy bouncing about of the modern 'offs' as they became known. No pushing the bloke in front of you into action in order to hide behind him. Just a demented, almost surreal, spontaneous orgy of physical butchery where everybody seemed to know their role.

I have to say that I have rarely seen violent disorder on that scale in any walk of life since and I, when I finally reached the safety of the London-bound train, mused to myself as to whether any mentally stable people did actually attend football matches in 1974. It then occurred to me that amidst all the carnage, I didn't even know who had won. The game had become completely immaterial. 1-0 to United, someone advised us. It seemed that most of those at the Station didn't know either as it transpired. Manchester United fans continued their status as a fearsome football gang but whereas so few modern 'hoolie' books ever actually tell the truth where opponent's successes are concerned, they had certainly met their match that day.

The sheer frenzied hatred of the Cardiff City fans as they came head to head with England's largest hooligan gang on that day was something to tell my grandchildren if I ever have any. In subsequent years, the two clubs fortunes varied drastically. Cardiff were destined for a lifetime in the lower leagues and United eventually found domestic and European glory but they were both top of the league on that August day.

The clubs' fans have had a varied history since. Cardiff evolved (maybe from that encounter) into one of the most notorious hooligan gangs, a stigma or accolade depending on your viewpoint that they hold to this day. United meanwhile have sadly been all but swallowed up by corporate greed. Their fans so often and highly unfairly pilloried as prawn-munching replica-shirt wearers from Singapore, (thanks to the incessant and somewhat successful PR campaign over the last 10 years chiefly from Manchester City's propaganda machine) yet even in those glory-less years, their nationwide support was unrivalled, highlighted on that day by a train full of 500 beer-swilling psychopaths heading back to Paddington.

So when newcomers to the game think that out-of-town Reds are a modern phenomenon created by success, I would laugh in their faces and know at an instant that they themselves are actually the very new-wave fans that they profess to despise. Whereas any clued-up match-going rivals who have been around longer than just the day after 'Three Lions' made the charts will know the score.

Post Euro '96 nouveau fans brought up on a diet of Fantasy Football, 606 phone-ins, Helen Chamberlain, Baddiel and Skinner wouldn't recognise the Manchester United of 1974 yet if one wanders around Salford or the City Centre on match day, especially when the likes of Leeds, Liverpool or Chelsea are due then anyone expecting to glimpse the stereotypical image of a United fan would be highly mistaken. Similarly United away games are beginning to see a return to the active followings of yesteryear, unrecognisable from the image portrayed by the type of United fan we all know, the office gimp who has 15 replica shirts but has never been to Old Trafford.

Cardiff fans continue to wreak havoc around the country and unlike United have never had an alternative image to have to shake off. Cardiff still know how to offer visiting fans that unique 'welcome in the hillside' but I doubt that anything would ever come close to that day in 1974. I doubt if anything could! Awful days, etched on my mind with a kind of fondness usually only reserved for cold school showers, or a kiss from an ugly Aunt. Yet strangely, they were wonderful times. At the time, it was an experience to chill the bones yet I wouldn't have missed it for the world.

When I finally returned home, unscathed, well at least physically, my Mum asked me if I had had a nice time in Wales. She probably imagined her little boy splashing around in the sea or acting the buffoon in the sand. I said it had been 'an interesting day'.

"Did you bring back any rock?" she asked. I thought back to the flying concrete at Ninian Park a few hours earlier.
"No, sorry," I replied, "there was plenty around but nothing I liked the look of."
"Never mind," said Mum, "as long as you've enjoyed yourself."
 I had been chased, spat at, terrified, seen men knocked unconscious and kicked senseless – yet she was right... I had!

From that day on, like many Cardiff fans too, I'm sure, I was hooked and followed United all over from that day on for over a quarter of a century. It's a funny kind of logic but in a way, although I reviled those 70's days of lawlessness and abject violence and terror and although it's best that they are consigned to history, I can't tell you how very glad I was that I was there. With fond memories to both Reds and Bluebirds".

Paul gives his view of the days events
"Excellent & accurate account of events that day. I was still in school at the time and I'll never forget the sight on entering the Grange end of a sea of red & white scarves on the Bob Bank. Pity that there was quite a number of lads from the same school as me standing on the Bob Bank. There's been a few incidents at fortress Ninian since, (Spurs '77, Chelsea '84) but nothing comes close to what happened that day. I'm personally glad things have moved away from the chaos of that era. The Leeds Cup Tie in 2002 was more like a vicar's tea party compared to events at grounds in those days. But of all the off's up and down the country, that crazy Saturday in Cardiff must be one of the most violent days in British football history."

Many of the Mancs who were there that day refer to this as 'The One day War' which from a firm who have been everywhere in the last 30 years and faced all comers, is a massive compliment to the Cardiff lads they met that day. This day's events is seen as the turning point at Cardiff and since then many teams have travelled to Cardiff and experienced the unique Welsh brand of hospitality. This story happened 34 years ago and Cardiff's hooligans are still going strong despite many jail sentences and police crackdowns. The potential for serious disorder still exists there.

D of The Barry Dockers version of Cardiff v Everton 70's
We all met at Barry Dock train station. This was a big game for us, Everton at home in the Cup. There was me, my brother, Donut, Orgy, Ivins, Sala, Bronson and his brother, Tata, Burkie, Veggie, Charlie and a few more Barry lads. We had originally intended to get off at Grangetown, but had heard that a few mobs of Scousers had been spotted in town so we stepped off at Cardiff Central and went looking for them. We had a few small off's around the place as we made our way to the ground then we plotted up in the Grange end to plan our attack on the Scousers in the Bob Bank.

The police were out in force so serious tactics would be needed in order to get at the Scousers. We spoke to the other various mobs of Cardiff including the Merthyr boys who we often teamed up with as they had a good mob of lads. We decided to move into the Bob Bank in small groups, two to four lads at a time so not to attract attention from the Old Bill. We said that once we are all in position, we would shout 'Barry Boys, we are here' and that would be the signal for mayhem. I could see the other boys were all in position so up went the chant. Everton didn't know what had hit them. They were running everywhere with us on them like a pack of wolves. They had special trains laid on at Ninian Park halt and you could see them scrambling, falling over and fighting each other in their panic to get on the train. A top day for us!

In the book **'Hooligans, an A to L of Britain's Hooligan Gangs' by Andy Nicholls,** an Everton fan tells how he took a savage kicking from Cardiff lads outside Central station and was then picked up off the floor and befriended by Veggie, a well known nutter of the time from Barry Island and taken to the Craddock Arms. He says when they went to the ground and Veggie found it to be full of Scousers, he was not impressed and immediately kicked it off, sparking mayhem. Another Everton fan says that many of them left before the game had ended but he stayed and said, "After the game, it was time to take a deep breath, keep your fucking head down and start the 30 minute walk of death to Cardiff Central".

Another old Barry Face PS tells of Cardiff's glory days of the 70's
People talk about the violent 80's but fuck me, the 70's was much, much worse. There was full scale war on the streets at some games. The police didn't have a clue nor did they give a fuck. They often used to say, "That way to the ground boys" and grin as they knew (or hoped) you were gonna get the cocky smile wiped off your face by the locals. When Leeds came to Cardiff, hundreds of us ambushed them on the bridge near Central and we kicked the absolute fuck out of them. They were jumping into the Taff to get away. It was that on top for them. So when we went there for the replay, we thought we were in for another day of 'bash the Northern fuckers'.

We came out of the train station, hundreds of us, no escort and not a copper in sight and marched down the road, cocky as fuck, thinking we were the daddys. All of a sudden it was like Zulu, as Leeds mob came at us from all sides. I shit myself as wave after wave of them steamed into us. I never thought any of us were gonna get out of it alive as this massive brawl went on forever and bodies lay in the gutter. It was like a war zone.

A funny story is the trip to **Bristol Rovers**. All the way to the ground it was kicking off with small groups and the police were getting really heavy handed with us. This copper on a horse was swinging his truncheon at people and shouting, "Move you Welsh cunts." My mate was smoking a fag and he put the fag out up the horses arsehole. The horse took off about hundred miles an hour with this wanker of a copper desperately trying to hang on.

Another time me and my mate were coming back from a game away, can't remember where. We pulled our car into the services and as we entered the Café we suddenly realised it was full of our old enemies, the **Swansea Jacks**. The Jacks have no qualms about battering small groups and started mouthing at us straight away because we had Cardiff scarves wrapped around our wrists. We made a sharp exit and as we walked back to the car, a coach of Valley Commandoes pulled in. We told them what had happened and they charged into the café and all we could see was Jacks legging it out the back and across a field. Lovely!

When **Villa** came to Cardiff they were outside the ground because they had been let out first and were busy throwing things over the wall into the ground. We ran down behind the Bob Bank and jumped the wall into the surrounding streets. We poured round to where they were and instant justice was dispensed on the Brummie bastards.

When **Chelsea** came, they were in one part of the Bob Bank and we were in another, separated by the police They were screaming and shouting and seriously pissing the police off. After a while the police just stepped to one side and said, "feel free" to us. 'Fuck me it's Christmas!' we thought as we steamed right into them. They were as game as fuck but we demolished them as our numbers were massive that day. When Chelsea came back in the early 80's, they had a mob and a half. The fighting went on in the backstreets around the ground well into the night, as hundreds of little mobs clashed for hours. House windows crashed in as the police lost control and basically shit themselves. This was the worst incident of football violence I have ever seen and was far worse than the Man Utd game of the 70's. Several people were stabbed in the carnage. The Chelsea mob that night were animals and so were we but we couldn't shift them no matter what. How nobody died that day is a mystery to me. It was pure savagery.

The so-called riot at the **Leeds** game where Sam Hammam walked around the pitch in recent years is a joke when compared to these incidents. These were the glory days of violence. I got out of the game as knives were taking it too far in my opinion and ruined it. But I'll always look back on these amazing days of the 70's with fond memories. Bloooobirds!

Simons version of Wales v Yugoslavia 76 and Cardiff in those days

"The ref Rudi Glöckner stitched up Wales, disallowing goals and all sorts. At the end of the game, the Welsh fans were so pissed off with a 1-1 draw, they smashed the fences down, invaded the pitch, attacked the Yugoslavian players and chased them down the tunnel and chased the ref with corner flags. It was mayhem.

At **Wales v England** '77, 200 English came on the Bob Bank and were absolutely slaughtered and had their silk scarves taken off them.

Another time around the same time, Cardiff went down to Swansea. They were having work done on the ground and you had to pay and walk through portacabins. The Cardiff fans en masse, pushed the portacabins to one side and everyone just piled in for free.

Worst place I ever went was **Tottenham** away around '77. They were everywhere. We could see them running in amongst the tower blocks trying to get to us. They kept Cardiff in for 45 minutes while the police battled to clear them away. This was the only time I've ever seen Doberman dogs used by the Old Bill.

In the early 80's we went to **Bristol Rovers** and were crammed in like sardines. A copper looked up and said, "Oh shit" as another special train full of Cardiff arrived. Next thing, the corrugated iron around the ground was being ripped back and more Cardiff were piling into the ground. It was mental. Afterwards Cardiff totally took the piss, spray painting cars, running through gardens, wrecking the place.

We went to Leicester and as we were escorted past the Rugby Ground near the ground, loads of them were there, mouthing and throwing things. Cardiff ran at them and after a few slaps they were on their toes. I couldn't believe it. I thought there was going to be a bloodbath but no, they just legged it. Top memories never to be repeated sadly."

Mike Bronson gives his view of the 70's scene:

"Due to the fact that a lot of the guys who shared my experiences are settled down and retired from the front line, I won't be using names here. They know who they are and I'm sure my memories of events will stir them. My first experience of the

Sion Aubrey Roberts – jailed
for sending letter bombs.

A cottage burns.
Welcome to the Hillsides
(above & right).

Me and Hobbsy aged 15 in
Harrington Jackets and Fred
Perry's.

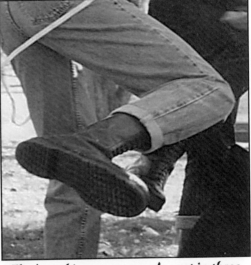

The last thing many people saw in those
days, a Doc Martin boot crashing into their
swede.

Still photos of a cowardly attack on a lone person by Skinheads.

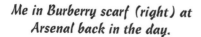

Retro Graffiti on the Station Bridge.

Barry Skins around 1980 (above).

Me in Burberry scarf (right) at Arsenal back in the day.

Fighting in Swansea's North Bank v Cardiff 80's (above).

Seasiders in the 80's (right).

Some of the old crew today (Me with the pie eater cap, 2nd left).

Lee Trundle waves the 'Fuck off Cardiff' flag.

Jacks in London (left) and protesting about a visit to Swansea by Looney Leftie MP George Galloway (below).

Why they have a Union Jack is anyone's guess !!!

TROUBLE BEFORE THE MATCH as a stone is thrown and a policeman moves into action.

Eight arrested at Vetch cup final

by Chris Peregrine

EIGHT soccer fans were arrested at last night's Welsh Cup final match between Cardiff and Wrexham at Swansea's Vetch Field.

But police said today that they were reasonably happy with the results of the operation they mounted.

And, local traders, who had been fearful of trouble between three sets of fans, praised the way police handled the situation.

Five Cardiff fans were arrested, two Swansea fans and a single Wrexham.

The arrests related to alleged public order offences inside or outside the ground and the eight have been bailed to appear in court at a later date.

BOISTEROUS

Police spokesman Inspector Bob Jones said today: "In general terms we are reasonably happy with the events of last night although the fans were extremely noisy and boisterous."

"They were pretty well behaved, with the exception of a few whose antics culminated in the arrests."

Eight buses were laid on by South Wales Transport to take the visiting Cardiff fans from

Swansea's High Street Station to the ground and back, for the two football special trains.

"It all went pretty smoothly," said SWT commercial director Mr. Alan Kreppel today. "All credit to everyone concerned."

"The police have got a lot of experience and policed it very well. There was no damage to any buses and I would like to thank our drivers and two inspectors."

A British Rail spokesman was not available to comment on reports that the football specials were delayed, causing chaos in Swansea because fans pulled communication cords on a number of occasions.

Vetch derby: extra police

EXTRA POLICE will be drafted into Swansea on Sunday when between 300 and 500 Newport County fans are expected for the Third Division soccer derby at Vetch Field.

The Newport fans will arrive by train and coach and police will be on duty in the city centre from early morning, head of Swansea Central police. Chief Superintendent Haydn Davies, said today.

When the two sides met at Somerton Park last October one Swansea fan was stabbed and 35 arrested as rival fans battled in the streets of Newport.

Swansea police will be taking precaution on Sunday to avoid another clash but they are not prepared to say what they are.

The police's barrier system will be in operation and the Newport fans will all be housed under the West Stand.

"We hope that everyone who goes to the match will do so to watch the game and enjoy it and that they won't spoil other people's enjoyment," said Chief Superintendent Davies.

Meanwhile, Chief Super-

intendent Davies yesterday met Swans' chairman Mr. Winstone Rees to draw up special plans to deal with any violence when London club Millwall visit the Vetch Field later this month.

Millwall are due to meet the Swans on March 26 although the fixture could be moved to another date.

Wales play Scotland the following evening and if there are any Swans players in the Welsh squad this could mean the Millwall game being postponed.

The top-level meeting between club and police followed the horrific scenes of soccer violence at Luton this week when Millwall fans ran riot.

On the first day of the soccer violence erupted between Millwall and Swansea fans at The Den — Millwall's ground — and the game was halted for 12 minutes when the fighting overflowed on to the pitch.

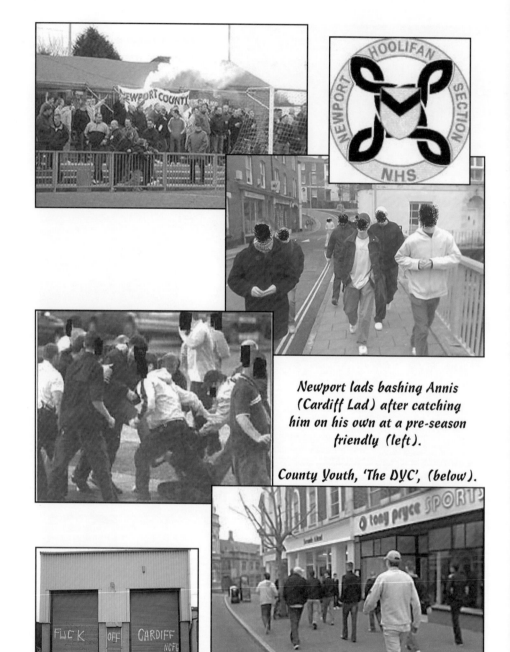

Newport lads bashing Annis
(Cardiff Lad) after catching
him on his own at a pre-season
friendly (left).

County Youth, 'The DYC', (below).

Lemmy in light shirt outside turnstiles at Cardiff, 80's (above) and Lemmy in more recent times (left).

Red Dragon Pub, Caia Park.

Caia Park Rioters on CCTV.

Calling Card

Chester fans arriving at Wrexham (right).

Wrexham at Wallsall (below).

CCTV Footage of Wrexham
attacking a pub in Chester
(left).

Barry Skins in the 70's (right)

and 70's Lads (below).

Skinheads with their
boots removed by Old Bill
(below).

1976 European Championship QF
Wales 1 Yugoslavia 1

Full time

WALES 1
EVANS 38

YUGOSLAVIA 1
KATALINSKI 19 pen

YUGOSLAVIA WIN 3 : 1 ON AGGREGATE

Cardiff at Bristol City early 80's (Skinhead days).

Cardiff waiting for Birmingham.

Wanted faces from the Stoke game (above),
Cardiff Youth (C-Squad) on CCTV in Coventry (left above).

Cardiff trying to get at Mancs.

Cardiff Boys in the 90's.

Cardiff lads in custody after the infamous Britania
pub battle in Plymouth.

Some Cardiff lads in Blackpool.

Hull at Ninian Park 2007 mouthing off behind Old Bill.

Soul Crew attempt to attack Rovers.

'BLOODY ANIMALS'

A SWANSEA city centre shop manager told today of the terror that hit the Quadrant when marauding football fans went on the rampage during peak Easter shopping time.

Mr. Benny Corbisero, manager of Gilesports, had to have seven stitches inserted in a hand wound after Cardiff City supporters kicked in the palte glass door of his hop.

And a city licensee described the fans as "bloody mindless animals."

A Swansea fan is kicked after being attacked by rival fans.

by Adrian Howells

through the centre," said Mr Cirbisero, who added that shopkeepers and shoppers were afraid throughout the day.

"The atmosphere was very tense, but I would like to praise the police. When this terrifying incident happened they expertly diffused what could have been an explosive situation," he added.

'Off the field, the result of Saturday's derby match between Swansea and Cardiff was 68 arrests, mass violence in the streets and a trail of damage to shops and pubs.

Deplorable

Cardiff City football club today condemned a "certain element" of their fans.

"The behaviour of some of them was deplorable and we as a football club do not want to be associated with them. Unfortunately this small element gives the rest of Cardiff City's genuine fans a bad name," said the club's managing director Mr. Ron Jones.

Blood streams from a head wound to a Swansea fan.

"Drink is the root cause of all these troubles and an early kick-off would mean the match being played before they can get drunk," he added.

"Unfortunately...scenes like those witnessed in Swansea is the unacceptable face of soccer," Mr. Jones said.

Kicked

It was the worst outbreak of soccer hooliganism to hit Swansea this season as violence flared in and around the city centre throughout the day and continued on the terraces at Veich Field during the match which Swansea won 3-2.

The Cornish Mount public

POLICE move the crowd from King's Lane, Swansea.

Britain's wildest derby.

Cardiff invade the pitch at Swansea 80's.

Cardiff over the moon as Jacks lose to Barnsley.

Cardiff 'en route' to Arsenal.

Merthyr Lads.

Cardiff arrive at Millwall.

Cardiff lads, 80's.

unity you feel being a part of a firm was one Bank Holiday when I saw the local Skinheads rucking with a gang of Hells Angels called the 'Road Rats'. These bikers were obviously experienced fighters but weren't prepared for the aggro from these lads who had been weaned on town in-fighting between different gangs (Colcot, Cadoxton, Barry Docks etc) and they came well unstuck. Admittedly it was the older generation who saw them off after they petrol bombed the Pele nightclub, but the bottle these youngsters showed impressed me a lot.

My brother had close links with these boys and was already into the football caper so I thought I'd give it a go myself. My memories dimmed a bit now but certain great days stay in my mind. Manchester United in Cardiff, there was this Downs Syndrome kid who always paraded round the front of the pitch wearing a copper's helmet. This day however, he was wearing a World War I tin helmet. Wise choice, as there were more missiles thrown than the siege of Leningrad. At the end of the game, Man Utd were gone but major fisticuffs went off back at Central station.

Swansea away. Every game against them was good fun. Say what you like about the Jacks but they were always up for it. They never won many against us. This particular game sticks in my mind because they had two papier-mâchè Swans on the pitch, big buggers. A Cardiff fan ran onto the pitch and proceeded to doggy fuck them. What a laugh! If I ever met that guy I'd gladly buy him a pint.

Grimsby away. We managed to get into their end before them and as they came through the turnstiles, we battered them. There ended up a big pile of unconscious bodies and we were all nicked, the whole coach load of us. At Millwall they were squirting petrol through the fences at us!

Leeds away. I'm not a fan of rail travel to matches. I always felt you were buggered before you started. Until Leeds that was. A full crew stepped on at Central. Good boys from Barry and Cardiff. At the time Leeds was being transformed so to get to the ground, you had to walk across a big building site for three miles. They came at us from all angles and it's off. The Old Bill came wading in on their horses and I saw a young lad get trampled and his thumb was hanging off. I was tossed to one side and bitten on the chest by one of these nags. The train home was like a mobile ambulance with blood and bandages everywhere.

The Home Internationals were a top laugh. Imagine all those Jocks, pissed up, bare arses everywhere and thousands of them. What I liked about them was, you could drink with them the night before, then on the Bob Bank the next day you'd be kicking fuck out of each other. One time we walked into a bar full of them and I had this cotton reel on me as I'd split my jeans in an earlier row. After a bit of banter, I threw this cotton reel at them and as I did the whole pub erupted. Tables, chairs, bottles, glasses all flying and we ended up outside. I was swinging this little pop bottle and was suddenly faced with this giant Jock in full Highland regalia. Now, discretion is the better part of valour so we re-grouped halfway down Ninian Park road (we ran like fuck).

Another top row was when thousands of **American soldiers** descended on the Island. The Barry boys came from everywhere and it went off all night. They were game as fuck but we gave it to them good. Respect to Havard and Dicko who were right involved.

The Barry boys had a good crew that you could always depend on. We even had a female gang that came with us, Janet, Dapper, Gail and Denise and they were game as well. There were some top Cardiff boys who could be relied on in a tight spot. There was Bubbles, Stabber, The Llanrumney boys but if you ask any of them including Frankie, they've all been glad to see the Valley Commandoes come charging over the hill to the rescue.

By far the best arena to show how good you were (or thought you were) was **Wembley** Stadium car and bus park. What a meeting of like minds that was! Every English club was represented there and a coach of Barry nutters to accommodate them. Top days.

Although the lure of the football has gone for me now and the only thing I kick these days is the telly, I still try to keep up with what today's boys are up to and I've been well impressed with the passion that's been shown to the cause over the years. The mobility of the different groups these days due to modern technology and communications amazes me and when the boys go abroad my heart goes with them. Up the City".

Kersy (one of the original Swansea Bay swimmers) tells of his first away trip, West Ham 1979.
"This was the first away game for me with my mates although I was a regular at home games. I was on King Square in Barry with Wally, waiting for the coach and the older boys turned up. The main boy at the time was Reggie and he said to us, "I hope you two have got your running daps on." We had no idea what he was on about. We had our Doc Martins on and thought we were the business. When our coach pulled up at Ninian Park, loads of skinheads and Punks were boarding

coaches and things looked good. As the coaches neared the ground in London, loads of West Ham were giving us the cut throat signs and we were all laughing at this. A few coaches of us pulled up at the same time and we were all walking towards a corner and everyone seemed to be hesitating. One of the older boys said, "C'mon, they'll think we are scared of them." As we turned the corner and crossed the road, West Ham piled out of the Boleyn pub, chucking glasses and anything else they could get their hands on. Everyone started running and West Ham were chasing us through the traffic. This was well on top! The police restored order and we had to walk back in the same direction again.

West Ham looked really evil but we eventually went through the turnstiles in one piece. Inside the ground, there was no segregation at all, only a thin line of Old Bill. It seemed like West Ham were bursting through every five minutes. After the game, me and Wally left early and climbed back on our coach. From the back windows, we could see pitched battles going on as the other Cardiff tried to get back to the coaches. The windows started coming in on the coaches and it was looking really heavy outside as both mobs constantly charged each other back and forwards.

On the way home we had the piss taken out of us for staying on the coaches while everyone else was fighting but we were only school kids and had shit ourselves. A few lads stepped on our bus bleeding everywhere after being hit by glasses outside the Boleyn earlier and I must say, I was glad to get out of that place alive!"

Chapter Nine
Cardiff's Soul Crew

As the 70's rolled into the 80's and the Casual culture took over, hooligan gangs started giving themselves names and Cardiff's became known as the Soul Crew. The name apparently comes from the Cardiff boys love of Northern Soul music and reportedly was made up by Nicky P, a far right geezer who then left Cardiff and went off to join Chelsea's Headhunters. They were more openly racist than the Cardiff lads, many of whom were from the Docks and didn't share his views. The Soul Crew has changed over the years with many faces coming and going. It contains people from as far apart as Neath, Port Talbot, Bridgend, Maesteg, Merthyr, Rhondda, Rhymney, Bangor, Holyhead, Newport, Llantwit, Penarth, Barry, in fact they come from all over Wales. Sometimes you won't see someone for five years then they suddenly reappear, as nuts as ever.

My Nightmare Trip
This story of my first football trip is from my other book but is needed to explain how I entered the football violence scene.

I went to the Marine one night in 1982 and at the end of the night I walked home with Wally and he said, "You like a bit of action, why don't you come to the football." I told him I wasn't into football and he said, "There's a coach to Millwall tomorrow, come on, you'll love it." I said I'd give it a go, nothing else to do. I'd never heard of Millwall before but apparently they were called the 'Bushwhackers' and the walk to the ground is called 'the murder mile'. When I stepped onto the coach at King Square, all the older, much more experienced boys, like Dickie Donut, Mike Bronson, Dessy etc were laughing at me and saying, "It's your first game and you're going to Millwall? Ha-ha." I just thought they were muppets.

When we arrived at the ground, we pulled into the car park and it was derelict wasteland, lonely and derelict. "Here we go," the older guys said. I still wasn't worried though as I didn't know what was going to happen. All of a sudden, we were surrounded by the biggest geezers I had ever seen, all dressed in Dockers donkey jackets and they were right in our faces shouting, "Is this a joke? Where's your big boys?" Our older boys steamed into them and a rambling fight went off. It was all over the place. I was absolutely terrified. We younger ones shuffled along and these psychos were all around us and every now and again they would smack one of us. They were just taking the piss out of us and there was nothing we could do. Dai Ellis jumps out and says, "I'm not having this. Let's do them." Smack - he's rolling down the bank getting kicked stupid. The whole thing goes mental and we are trying to fight back but it's useless.

At that very second, two more coaches of Cardiff's older boys pull in and there's mayhem. Kersy gets bitten by a police dog and two coppers are in the middle of it scared out of their wits and lashing out at anyone with truncheons. Me and Wally run and get to some sort of shelter. We pick up bricks to defend ourselves but we don't know whose who and there's now hundreds of people fighting all around us and bricks were flying through the air. We run to the turnstiles and everyone's scrambling to get through as bricks bounce off the wall about our heads. I remember Dai Ellis saying, "I haven't any money to get in. Someone lend me £2.50." I remember seeing a sign which said anyone taking weapons or missiles into the ground will be banned. My heart sank. What was I doing here? Why hadn't I stayed in bed? It was too late though. I was here. This was real and we're all going to die!

In the ground Millwall were in the next enclosure. Panda pop glass bottles were raining down on us, darts were flying through the air and a black pool ball was thrown back and forth all through the game. Millwall were singing 'We are evil' over and over and I was shitting bricks. In the middle of all the fighting, a game of football broke out. At half-time, a load of older Cardiff came into the ground, some covered in blood, all excited saying they had done Millwall on the tubes. I think we beat them 4-0 and it was looking really bad for us now! The final whistle goes and they let Millwall out and keep us in for 20 minutes. "Here we go," I think, "We're dead for sure now." We come out and Millwall are nowhere to be seen. "They've bottled it they don't want to know now we are all together," we thought.

Our 13 coaches take off and I'm falling asleep against the window as we've been driving through London for about 15 minutes. All of a sudden the windows on the coach are caving in and we are surrounded by hundreds of Millwall. We're lying on the floor as more and more bricks hit the coach. One of the older guys called Noddy opens the exit and says, "Let's do 'um." If you jumped off the coach, that would have been the end of you. "Fuck that." I'm not getting off but we started throwing bottles and cans out of the broken windows at them. We were putting our sleeves over our hands, grabbing handfuls of broken window glass and spraying that at them.

Next thing Millwall are having running battles with the Police and one big black guy runs up a walkway and jumps off it. It's about 40 foot high. He hits the deck, rolls, gets up and legs it. Loads of Millwall are nicked. A copper comes on the coach and asks if we can identify any of them. One of the older guys says, "The leader only had one eye, in the middle of his forehead." We all roared with laughter. We weren't interested in pressing charges or helping the police, just wanted to get home in one piece.

As all the coaches were wrecked, they took us all to pubs to wait for new coaches. Cardiff absolutely trashed the pubs. We were behind the bars helping ourselves to beer and spirits. One guy is throwing crisps and fags out into the crowd like a crazed barman on acid. Millwall are all around shouting stuff but there aren't enough of them to attack again so we just laugh at them now. Eventually we get back on the coaches and away. Now, all day I've been saying to myself 'never again' but on the way home I realised, although I had shit myself and I'd never been so scared in my life, I had actually loved it. It was better than sex and I was hooked.

Now it was game on, I was up for the football big time. In the middle of all that mayhem, the possibilities were endless. Everywhere you went, it kicked off. Wally and Kersy who had been going to the football since they were kids, explained it to me. I'd never been interested in football and I wasn't interested now but I could see that football was an opportunity to involve myself in the ultimate gang war. Arsenal, Bristol, Chelsea, Reading, Newport, Wrexham, Swansea, all the shitty Northern clubs and every time there was a guaranteed battle. I was loving it.

As the 80's moved on, the firms became more organised and dangerous. Stanley knives became the weapon of choice for many firms. We heard stories of Chelsea, Everton, Liverpool and West Ham slashing up people. This led to a lot of our boys carrying them too and horrific injuries followed all over the country.

Have you met Stanley?
The carrying of weapons is a vicious circle and even if you have a blade simply to scare people off if you are cornered, inevitably you will end up using it. When Jerky slashed a Newport fan, causing him to need 200 stitches, he was jailed for 2 years. A Brummie who slashed one of our boy's faces received 2 years and I stabbed 2 Mancs and had 2 years. This sort of sentence was dished out a lot during the 80's but these days, you would be looking at five years and up. Hopefully these nasty tools are left where they belong, in the past. You don't hear a lot about blades at the footie these days although a Manc was slashed by Cardiff a few years ago but

his attackers, when arrested turned out to be 11 and 13!

Chelsea

In the 70's and 80', Chelsea caused Cardiff's mob more grief than anyone else. Turning up in massive numbers and taking on all-comers. One of the Cardiff lads 'C' tells the story of their raid on Cardiff in the early 80's.

"It was kicking off all through the game. It was mental. Outside the Chelsea hordes were taking it to Cardiff big time. The Cockneys were very organised unlike us and they were smashing Cardiff and Valleys lads all down Sloper road. At the time I was 17 and was terrified. Every time Cardiff grouped up to go back into them, they were going through us like an army unit. Even though we had some fucking hard boys with us, we couldn't deal with their numbers and organisation. We regrouped in massive numbers under the tunnel by the Ninian Pub and they came back at us. I could see their front line were all blokes in their 30's and try as we might, they just beat us back. Some of the older guys were so frustrated, I swear they had tears in their eyes. A few Cardiff were stabbed up as well which made the whole day much more frightening. It was the worst mob I've ever seen at Ninian. Hats off to them."

Hartlepool United Away by Meic Gough

(Author of Patches, Checks and Violence published by www.lulu.com)

It was the mid 80's and another new season was looming. First up was a trip to the North East of England. The lads had been talking about this trip since the fixtures came out. The first away trip is always a bit special and this game was going to be a little different because at the time Ayresome Park, the home of Middlesbrough FC was out of use so, after our game, Boro were playing Port Vale at the same stadium and an opportunity arose for the Soul Crew to go head to head with the Frontline.

Opening day fixtures were also a chance to meet up with old mates and catch up on all the holiday brawls and mayhem that each other had been involved in. This was a new ground for myself and also the furthest. Only Dukey had travelled further. He was a couple of years older and had been to both Newcastle and Sunderland. Around this time the favoured mode of transport was the Service train and the Soul Crew were taking at least 200 lads to every away game. Britain was in the midst of recession and the train fare was well out of our price range. We left it until the evening before the game to get a 14 seater minibus sorted and at chucking out time we left the Black Crown boozer in Porth and headed for the North. Dean, Cen,

Ashley, Ronnie Rock, Dukey, his mates Budgie and Jeff from Cardiff plus myself all fitted out in the latest Casual labels. There wasn't a qualified driver amongst us. We managed to blag the minibus on Blakey's license, luckily there was no photo ID in those days. Budgie did the driving but we very rarely reached over 60 mph as we slowly covered the miles.

We arrived in **Hartlepool** around 8:00am and parked up close to the train station. The lads on the train were due in around 9:30am so we headed for breakfast to kill time. Full to the brim on bacon and sausages, we headed back to the station. We didn't have to wait long. As the train pulled in, lads came jumping out of the doors; a sea of Pringle jumpers and wedges. We met up with a couple of our mates from the Rhondda who had managed to jump the train. Four of them huddled in the cramped bog for the majority of the journey. Fuck that I thought. Their journey had been much more fruitful than ours. They had changed trains in Darlington and on the opposite platform were 70 Darlo lads. Both firms went for each other. Our lot had slightly the greater numbers and as the rival firms met, our lot smashed through Darlo's frontline. This split their firm in two as half their number legged it out of the station. Those that stood were rounded on and given a good hiding before they too beat a hasty retreat. All too soon the familiar sight of the Old Bill turned up and they escorted Cardiff back to their platform and ensured there was no more nonsense.

We made our way out of Hartlepool station. Spirits were high, around 120 of us. We made our way to the town centre but it wasn't long before the Old Bill were on the scene so a small group of us went back to the minibus. Budgie decided to park up close to the stadium and we didn't bump into the train lads again until kick-off.

Time dragged by ever so slowly. The boozers didn't open until midday so the lads spent their time taking turns to drive the minibus around a large playing field. Finally the boozers opened and we found a large pub close to the ground with a pool table and Jukebox. Hartlepool looked a rough old town; very industrialised with a lot of big blokes mooching around. Dukey and Budgie were playing pool against a couple of locals who informed us that a mob of 50 Boro were in town early and had given some Hartlepool lads a slap. All the talk in the boozer was of revenge. This afternoon was going to be interesting to say the least. We left the boozer close to kick-off time and our small group split up. Cen, Dean, Ashley and I went in the Away End, Budgie and Jeff joined Rawlins, Woodsy and a dozen others in the Grandstand and Dukey and Ronnie Rock we didn't see again until the following Wednesday.

The atmosphere in the ground was friendly and before the game we even managed to invade the pitch for a kick about. The local Old Bill were laid back and happy to share a laugh and a joke with the travelling Blue Army. The Away End was full. Around 1500 Cardiff had made the long trek North consisting of 200 lads including Oz, Biten and Turkey from Hopkinstown plus Bunjy from Ynysybwl who was spending the weekend in the locality. The game was no more than 10 minutes old when the friendly atmosphere was shattered. A mass brawl erupted in the Grandstand sending innocent supporters fleeing to safety. Twenty of our lot and equal numbers of Hartlepool slugged it out. Punches flew from both sides and a couple of lads were knocked over the wooden seats and were mercilessly stamped upon. Both groups gave as good as they got with winners and losers on both sides. A big blonde lad was covered in blood and his Polo shirt was in shreds and then suddenly, it was over. The Old Bill were dragging lads out of the Stand and out of the ground. This outbreak of violence pumped up the atmosphere. It was electric but it wasn't over yet. The game itself was played out as a goalless bore draw with very little incident but that could not be said for what was happening off the pitch. With 10 minutes before the end, a mob of a 100 lads stormed the Hartlepool end. Clearing it, they then made their way towards us. These were Boro. Both sets of lads attempted to get at each other but the Old Bill somehow managed to keep both firms at bay. At the final whistle, we steamed out into the street only to be met by hundreds of Boro being escorted towards the ground. We had no choice but to pass each other and punches were swapped with the Boro lads. The Old Bill had their hands full with lads steaming in and out of the escort and only the sharp smack of the truncheon kept the warring factions apart.

The police split the Cardiff into two groups - Service Train and Coaches. We made our way with the Coach crowd and found our minibus which had been attacked by Boro. We had no choice but to sit and wait for our driver Budgie who had the keys. Groups of Boro hung around the entrance of the car park and picked off groups of Cardiff stragglers. Jeff returned to the minibus and told us Budgie had been nicked for his part in the row in the stand so we left the minibus and made our way to the police station where we learned that 20 Cardiff and 15 Hartlepool plus 30 Boro had been nicked and were all being banged up until Monday when they would go in front of a special court. We managed to get the Minibus keys from Budgie and once we were reunited with the van, Ashley took up the mantle and drove us home. Because of the damage to the van, we lost our £100 deposit which was a bitter pill to swallow.

Hereford United Away

Around the early to mid 80's, Cardiff City were a yoyo club and spent many seasons in the Third and Fourth Divisions and around this time we played Hereford quite regularly. They were at the time a kind of local rival. I always enjoyed away trips to Hereford. It was quite easy to get to, there were plenty of boozers and Hereford always had an active firm. I have been to Hereford on numerous occasions but one in particular stands out. Because of previous violent encounters between the rival firms, the Old Bill were starting to get smart and were closing all the local boozers before the game. This was when all kick-off times were 3:00pm on a Saturday not like nowadays when you have to play midday on a Sunday plus a Coach and Ticket Bubble Trip thrown in for good measure.

We decided we would still travel by Service train but get off in Leominster - one stop after Hereford for a swig. The platform at Cardiff Central was rammed with lads and just a sprinkling of Transport Police. Cen, Ashley, Oz, Bitten, Turkey and I all waited to board the 9:00am train. There must have been over 300 lads present including two dozen blokes from the Valleys who I always travelled with. We boarded the train and headed for the rear compartment where we kept our heads down while others played fuck with the buffet car. The lads were very mischievous that day. We pulled into Abergavenny and half the train emptied and the lads rampaged off through the streets of the quiet market town. The 30 of us carried on with our journey, all with tickets to Leominster but we knew that Hereford station would be awash with Old Bill so we would have to keep a low profile. We also knew that the 120 lads that would depart at Hereford would keep them busy. The plan worked a treat and we carried on our merry way. At Leominster, we holed up in a boozer close to the station. We planned to leave Leominster an hour before kick-off and enter Hereford's town centre undetected and smash any hostile resistance that we came into contact with.

We arrived back at Hereford station only to be confronted by 50 Old Bill who were pissed off that we had put a spanner in their works. They intended to make us pay. Firstly they manhandled us off the train and then lined us up against the station wall and searched us thoroughly. They then proceeded to push us across the road and any objections were met with a swift sharp dig with a truncheon but they weren't going to have it all their own way. We too were gutted. Our bit of fun had been well and truly fucked up and we weren't going to go to the ground quietly. The 30 of us pushed the pace of the escort and shoved the Old Bill up the street and when the police line was stretched we tried to make a run for it. Summers and Foster were the first to leave the escort and made their way through the cemetery with a couple of Old Bill hot on their heels. The remainder of us were taken up a steep hill into the town where we passed a group of a dozen Hereford lads who made their way into the middle of the road. A couple of our lot confronted them but we couldn't get within a couple of yards of them. They shadowed our escort through the town and towards the ground before disappearing. Once the ground was within sight, the Old Bill released their stranglehold on us and we were allowed more freedom. Once at Edgar Street we were pushed towards the large away terracing but we had other ideas. We were going in the stand or so we thought. Once again we felt the heavy hand of the Old Bill as we were beaten towards the turnstiles. We were told to get in the away end or fuck off back on the train. Fuck this I thought and headed away from the ground. I hoped a couple of the lads would join me but they all entered the ground.

Walking back towards the town centre, I met a group of Cardiff lads who weren't that interested in the game and we decided to have a couple of quiet pints and maybe catch the second half. We arrived on the main street and there opposite were the Hereford lads from earlier. Equal numbers, no police, this was it. Both groups made for each other, the mandatory standoff and then BANG! We were into them. The first that came my way was a lad in a hooded leather jacket and I stuck a couple of swift punches into his head. Another one of theirs was knocked over the bonnet of a parked car and fell at my feet so he got a boot in his chops. It was going off all around me and we managed to push them back across the road. A couple of their lot were floored in the first encounter but still the battle raged. One Hereford lad was forced into a shop doorway and was set upon by a couple of our lot. He was beaten to the ground and given a good shoeing. There were still six of them on their feet and again we charged them. They stood at first but after a couple of punches and boots, they split and after another brutal assault they scattered. One ran past me and I managed to catch him to the side of his head and he weaved his way up the road to safety. A couple of our lot still wanting blood sped after them but the majority of us had had our fill. We agreed it was too risky to have a pint and we returned to the ground.

Inside the ground I was reunited with Keith, Rees, Adie, Mike Robson, Wayne, Steve Eckhardt, Bexy and the others. There must have been 2,500 travelling fans. We filled all behind the goal and the atmosphere was electric and the cross-border hatred spewed from the terraces.

At the final whistle, we steamed out onto the street and headed for the Home End while the straight heads went to locate their coaches and cars. The main road outside Edgar Street was awash with 500 Cardiff hooligans and amid this chaos were innocent supporters of both teams milling around attempting to reach the car parks. Also on the mooch were groups of Hereford and sly punches were thrown from both sides. The Plod finally restored order and started to escort us back to the train station. The escort must have consisted of 2,000 blokes. There were 12 riot vans at the front and rear plus dog handlers. The only thing missing was the horses. The escort moved at a snail's pace and anyone who tried to speed up or slip away was given a whack with some wood but this didn't stop them trying. We headed down the hill by a church. Still penned in like sardines and the pace still being dictated by the Plod when suddenly a mob of around a hundred Hereford appeared at the bottom of the hill. Everybody surged forward forcing the Old Bill to draw their truncheons. Onward we pushed and some coppers were knocked over and on we went down the hill, the surge gathering momentum. We smashed our way through the police line and they were forced to call for reinforcements. The Old Bill were losing control and on we went, ever closer to Hereford's mob who didn't seem to be making any attempt to get to us. Unperturbed on we went. In the carnage were coppers and lads alike strewn across the road. We were nearly onto them but still Hereford did nothing. The Old Bill battled to halt us and finally in desperation they let the dogs off their leashes and they tore into us like they hadn't been fed for weeks. Their vicious fangs locked onto anyone in their path and finally the surge was ceased. Some of our lot encircled a couple of dogs and gave them a kicking but on large the dogs backed us off and enabled the Old Bill to regain control.

The escort came to a stop. The Old Bill filled the road ahead of us and the Hereford were herded away from the area. We proceeded to the station where a twenty carriage Football Special awaited us which was soon filled. Sat in the crowded compartments were lads with heads split open and wounds from dog bites and my mate Summers had had his bollocks bitten.

The train finally set off bound for Wales but it wasn't long before the locals were pelting the windows with rocks and a couple of lads had their heads split open. The train resembled a war zone and when we arrived at Cardiff Central, there were fleets of ambulances to ferry the injured to local hospitals. I have been to Hereford several times since then and although there is always violent disorder there has never been anything on that scale.

At the end of the 80's the whole scene seemed to die a death as rave culture and E's (Ecstasy tablets) swept the country. Suddenly all the lads from the different firms were raving and partying with each other. This loved up bollocks was doomed to fail though and a lot of Cardiff's lads slowly drifted back to their old ways.

Here's 'N's version of Bristol City v Cardiff in early 90's

We travelled to Bristol on a football special (cheap train laid on by the club). At least 1200 lads all crammed in like sardines. The police held up the train at Temple Meads station to avoid us causing the usual chaos but this just delayed the inevitable. We poured off the train and out of the station. The Old Bill were three deep blocking the exit but there were so many of us, we just swept them aside and ran off down the road in search of Bristol. During the pushing and shoving I was forced towards a wall with metal spikes sticking out of it. I remember thinking 'shit this is gonna be painful' as I fell towards it. As I was heading for the spikes, I instinctively grabbed someone and held them in front of me. Luckily it was a copper who screamed as he crashed into the metal spikes.

The long walk to Ashton Gate was uneventful apart from the fact that every pub we came to had smashed windows which was greeted by cheers from us. Apparently the boys on the earlier train had attacked their main pub only to be beaten back by a 150 strong mob of Bristol after a vicious exchange.

As we approached the ground, the silly Worzels inside the ground were singing, "Is that all you take away?" and a few of them were foolishly hanging around outside the away end. The first Worzel copped an umbrella over his head and the rest were kicked and punched all over the place. We entered the ground and our number had soared to 2,700. Bristol had sussed out a few Cardiff in their end and chased them towards us. We surged towards the gate in an attempt to force it open which caused the Bristol to backtrack.

A late winner gave Cardiff a 1-0 win and that's when the fun really began. 200-300 Bristol started attempting to invade the pitch. The Old Bill were all along the Cardiff end stopping us from going over the top. Coins, bottles and even crutches were thrown at the Bristol fans. As the final whistle sounded, the Bristol fans started bombarding Cardiff with masonry from behind our stand. We surged towards the big steel gates and ripped them open. Toe-to-toe fighting broke out just outside the ground but Bristol had no chance and although they really wanted it, they ended up running like gazelles.

The police tried to restore order but they were beaten back by concrete blocks, steel poles and corrugated iron roofing being ripped off and thrown by a howling

Cardiff mob. Order was only restored when the Cardiff firm decided they had had enough. The newspapers the following day condemned the Cardiff fans behaviour and said it was 'worse than Millwall'. There's no greater compliment.

B's version of Hull away around '95

"We met at the 1927 Café in Splott early doors. We had a minibus with a few characters like Mac, etc in it and a few cars full of headers as well. We set off on the long gruelling journey to Boothferry Park. We knew they had a game little mob and as we had arrived early for a night match, we plotted up in the nearest pub to the car park and waited for Hull to show up. We had dismantled a few stools and hidden the legs behind a door in case they outnumbered us when they came. They didn't come. After the game, we drove around looking for them and couldn't find anyone that wanted to know anywhere. Total waste of time. We went back there in 2005 and this time there was a big crowd. They clearly had a lot of boys in the ground. Outside, Cardiff started ripping down the fences and it kicked off a bit but we were beaten back by Old Bill on horses. The Hull that were there didn't really seem that up for it and I know that they are better than that. They have a good reputation so I was quite surprised really. It's a hell of a long way to go for fuck all to happen."

Sly Bastards, Man City Away '98 by Annis Abraham Jnr

Author of 'Diary of The Real Soul Crew' and 'From Shattered Dreams To Wembley Way'

Now I'd been to Man City a couple of times during the 80's and they've always had a good turn out and to be honest, it's been even Stevens between us and them in the past. Cardiff were once again back in the dungeon league (Div 4) so the forthcoming season as usual was nothing to get excited about. The usual pre-season friendlies came up with nothing of major interest then, with about three days notice, a friendly was arranged at Man City on a Thursday night on the 30th July 1998. It was arranged hastily and had something to do with compensation for Phil Neal walking out on us. A few phone calls were made but most of the lads were either on holidays or had other plans. So no more than 40 lads were expected to go which was unthinkable for Cardiff. On the day of the game, five of us left in the car, namely Frankie, Patrick, Emlyn, Topman and myself. We left about lunchtime and a few other car loads were expected to follow later. On the way up, a mate of mine, Lakey, phoned to say four or five other car loads were following but wouldn't be there until about 7:00pm.

We arrived about 5:00pm and as we were driving towards Maine Road, we passed a pub on the left hand side with about 20-30 lads outside and probably many more inside. We continued to drive and found a quiet pub about ¼ of a mile from Maine Road. From there we rang the other Cardiff to say where we were. We knew we couldn't go for a wander because what could five lads do? By 7:15pm no one else had arrived so we drove the car to the ground and ended up parking in some infant school car park called St Edwards. We thought that it was probably the safest place to leave the car. As we walked to the ground, the streets were quite empty and hardly any Old Bill around. It's the same old story when there isn't any Old Bill; if only our lads were out tonight.

We entered the virtually empty stadium and found that our end was as bad as the rest of the stadium. We had no more than 20 lads and 80 fans. The atmosphere was shit and the game was no better. Come half time, five of the lads even went home. Then suddenly out of the blue, two lads walked along the side of the pitch and straight up into our stand behind the goal eventually making their way to us. "All right lads," came the voice from a lad in a white jacket for which he then continued with "We've only come over for a chat. We've had about 80 lads out waiting for you lot since about 4:00pm." With that, we told him, "As you can see, no one's come." For the next half an hour he rambled on and it seemed like he wanted to be our best mate, even asking us if he could go to Anfield to see some of Wales's games as he hated Scousers so much. Before he went, he shook all our hands and even exchanged phone numbers with one of the lads.

At the end of the game we walked out of the away end and split up as our cars were in different directions. The car parks at Maine Road are massive and it was about 9:45pm and half the lights weren't even on. The crowd had been so low there weren't even any Old Bill standing outside our end; just a van by the side of the gates. As we walked across the car park, there were some coaches to our left taking Man City fans back to their areas. Next thing we knew, shouts of, "Come on" came from the left by the coaches. About 50 Man City lads had hidden themselves away for a sly attack and guess who was leading them - the lad in the white coat who had just spent half an hour trying to be our best mate. I remember Topman saying to me, "What shall we do now?" I said, "If we run, we'll end up scattered all over the place and battered, just stick together and keep walking." The walk was now virtually a trot and we were all now shitting ourselves. We knew we were dead meat if we clashed with them. "Where are the Old Bill when you need them," shouted Emlyn. I replied, "Don't worry Emlyn. For once, they're here," as a van drove straight into the middle of the car park with its flashing lights on. Once again I said, "Don't run, try and show them we're not wankers like them."

Man City continued to come towards us with the van swerving into them on several occasions. By now we could see my car ahead. I said to everyone, "Don't go near it as I'd rather take a few punches then get my car wrecked." We slowed right down as if we were making a stand. I shouted at the two faced Man City lad, "What a wanker you are, 50 onto 5." Then three coppers jumped out of the van with their truncheons out and waded into Man City. Man City were now all over the place with the coppers hitting them back. We decided to go nowhere and stood near the coppers. Just as it looked like it was totally coming on top, a couple more vans arrived to our relief to which we then eventually made our way to the car.

Unbelievable we said to each other. Usually on a game like this we would have had hundreds of lads. Patrick tried to ring the sly Man City fan but he had turned off his phone. That night I thought Man City were well out of order and in the past I had had a lot of respect for them. I suppose it's our fault for having so low numbers yet a few weeks later at a mid week league game at Shrewsbury Town, we had over 400 lads. What a joke.

Millwall at Home 1999
The turnout for this game was unbelievable. Boys were out in town who hadn't been involved in football violence for years. There must have been 2000 thugs on the streets of Cardiff. This day was, in my opinion, when a lot of boys came back

Rival fans escorted by police

POLICE supplied an escort for supporters from Cardiff city centre to Ninian Park after trouble flared on Saturday.

Officers took the decision in the wake of a disturbance in the city centre in which supporters from both teams clashed in the hours leading up to the match.

More than 100 police officers were drafted in to provide extra security for the Division Two clash.

The disturbances forced organisers of the Lord Mayor's Parade to direct the procession away from the Hayes area of the city centre where many of the Millwall supporters were gathered.

A police spokeswoman said no arrests were made in the early disturbances. "There were a few skirmishes and because of this we had to direct the Lord Mayor's parade, but

POLICE ESCORT *Police herd fans through Caroline Street, Cardiff, and, inset, how the police* into the scene. When about 90 of Millwall's 'Bushwackers' came off the train, they had the shock of their lives. They were hit with bricks, bottles and massive numbers of Taffies were all baying for their blood. At the ground, they came under constant bombardment of stones and coins and foolishly forced open a back gate at the ground. They came out into the worst mob of Cardiff ever assembled. This has been written about many times but at the risk of repeating this, they received the hiding of their lives. At least they came down and showed they were up for it which is more than a lot of people have done.

Around the same time as Wembley was being knocked down, the decision was made to play all big games at the Millennium Stadium in Cardiff. This meant all the big teams would be coming to Cardiff with inevitable results.

Report of Manchester United v Liverpool 2001

Cardiff supporters returning from their match against Wycombe found the Prince of Wales pub full of Manchester United fans who were in town for the Charity Shield the next day. Police kept the two groups apart against a barrage of missiles and the hooligans fought running battles with police throughout the evening. 22 people were arrested including two Cardiff youths aged just 11 and 13 after a Manchester fan was slashed down his back and a police officer suffered a broken arm. There was more violence before the Charity Shield game the next day when a 50 strong mob of Liverpool and Cardiff fans allegedly attacked Manchester followers in the city centre. This was also a time when an undercover journalist was with the Cardiff fans. The undercover reporter Jason Williams said:

"It was looking the part that concerned me more. To pass as a football hooligan, I had to look like one and that meant wearing the right kind of gear. There is a fascination among football hooligans with designer labels such as Lacoste, Burberry, Aquascutum and in particular with Italian label Stone Island. Having trawled the designer shops, I felt confident that I would at least be accepted as a 'lad' - a term football hooligans use amongst their peers. Unfortunately for them, their taste in clothes can be their undoing. I was turned away from a pub in Cardiff on one occasion. Ironically, it was not for wearing a football shirt but for wearing Stone Island because of its association with hooligan culture.

The town is home of Cardiff City's notorious 'Soul Crew', one of the top hooligan firms in Britain. I was there on the opening weekend of the season for the Charity Shield. Being an Englishman, I knew it would be difficult to convince them that I was one of their own. But somehow my Welsh accent passed the test. Armed with my secret camera, I had been with them throughout the day as they searched for trouble. We roamed the back streets of Cardiff looking for Manchester United fans and trying to avoid the police.

"Can you smell that?" one said looking straight at me. "I can smell fucking English."

For an instant, I thought my cover was blown. Luckily his comments were not aimed at me. There was no more trouble that day. I was able to leave without being caught out by this violent group."

There were several confrontations between Mancs and Cardiff lads and in the book 'Men in Black' the author who says they've never been done says, "We chased Cardiff across the bridge and I told the young ones not to go too far across, but they did and a load of massive Taffies caught them. I steamed back into them. We did ok for a bit but were then overwhelmed by them." Now maybe I've got it wrong here but being overwhelmed and being done are the same thing aren't they? Well that's Mancs for you. Another brawl that night was with the Barry Dockers lads at Poets Corner where he says Cardiff a slap but the lads that were there say different.

When Birmingham played Liverpool at the Millennium Stadium, the message boards were red hot with threats and counter threats. One Cardiff idiot wrote "What's the plan for the Brummies coming down? We must put up some resistance." The night before the game, the Zulus clashed with Cardiff lads all over town. One of the Gabalfa lot was stabbed in the lip by a black Zulu in St Mary Street and now looks like he has a hair lip. A TV Documentary was shown on the weekends events, with footage of Cardiff lads attacking a pub full of Zulus.

D tells the story
"We knew the Zulus were in the pub and we also knew that the first fuckers through the door will most likely get hurt as allsorts will be flying. We were all 'charlied up' and didn't give a fuck. Straight through the door we went, about 20 of us in the front line. I was hit by glass after glass then chairs and ashtrays as they stood at the back and just let us have it. One of ours was crawling out on his hands and knees across broken glass and was cut to ribbons. I know it was stupid but it had to be done. They had to know that if you come to Cardiff, we are here and we will be having a go at you. Fair play to Birmingham, they had an excellent mob and were right up for it. Hats off to them."

The Worzels - Report on Bristol City v Cardiff City 2001

The Cardiff 'Soul Crew' hooligans were escorted to the Coliseum pub. From there they were taken to Ashton Gate. Small groups of Bristol City hooligans were in touch by mobile phone to their Cardiff rivals. They tried to attack the escort at Ashton Park but were held back by the police. After the game, 40-50 Bristol hooligans attacked Cardiff fans as they left the ground. There was hand to hand fighting before police horses charged in. This whole incident was captured on video as we had an undercover journalist from the BBC with us, slyly filming us. The video of this can be seen on www.youtube.com/watch?v=y7WJmxmpxd4.

Here's Ds version of this day

"We were on the train to Worzel-land early. We figured that if 30-40 of us could get there, we could find the Worzels before the Old Bill cottoned on. Wrong! As soon as we stepped off the train, we were Section 60'd (searched for weapons) and then marched to a nearby pub. Throughout the day more and more Cardiff arrived and we were all penned in, drinking with a load of Old Bill around us. Some Worzels phoned us and said they would attack the pub and if we went for it too, the Old Bill wouldn't have enough to stop it. This never happened though. I think Bristol did probably make some sort of attempt to get there because all of a sudden, the Old Bill went from being ok to coming in really heavy handed. They screamed at us that we were leaving the pub and being escorted to the ground. We didn't fancy that much so we refused and started smashing up the pub.

On the way to the ground, we smashed up cars and the funniest part was when we passed these grotty tower blocks and were all singing 'You're Gypos 'til you die' at all the vermin hanging over the balconies. Some of them were throwing shitty nappies down at us, the fucking animals. As we passed a park, a bottle whizzed past my head and some young Worzels ran through the bushes throwing bricks at us. A big roar went up and it was obvious there was a large mob in the darkness of the park. Some of us went over the wall into the unknown but fighting erupted as the Old Bill fought to keep us out and chased the Bristol back through the bushes.

As we approached the ground, we could see scuffles kicking off in the distance as small groups of Cardiff were being attacked. A few of ours were across the road and into the fuckers and although they were game, they took some serious punishment from some of our big lads. After the game there was mayhem as Bristol mingled in with us and it was kicking off everywhere. The main escort was attacked and it went right off for a while. You could see the police were scared. They were losing control. All in all a top day out. Just like going back to the 80's. A few of our fans who went up by car found Worzels waiting by their cars and were CS gassed which was a bit naughty. City have some good lads but they also have a lot of cunts who will happily attack scarfers which they showed when they recently terrorised **Stoke** who hadn't taken any mob at all, just families and shirters. But then I suppose that's the way it happens these days. There's no respect anymore."

Quote: "I don't fear returning to Elland road with Man Utd. You seem to forget I played at Ninian Park last season." *Rio Ferdinand*

Cardiff City v Bristol City 2001

The Bristol City hooligan group of around 300 was escorted from the Old Monk pub to the ground. On the way they were attacked by Cardiff lads near Grangetown Station. The police baton charged the Cardiff hooligans. During the game coins, cans and bottles of urine were thrown by both sides. Cardiff hooligans racially abused Bristol City fans (English cunts, etc) and ripped up and threw seats.

"Always shit on the English side of the Bridge" (top chant)

After the game, Bristol fans returning to their cars and coaches were pelted with stones and found tyres slashed. Cardiff hooligans then fought with police for up to an hour. A local photographer was kicked unconscious. Little did the Cardiff boys realise that the whole thing was still being secretly filmed by an undercover journalist for the BBC's Hooligans programme.

Cardiff v Bristol Rovers

The Rovers mob arrived in Cardiff early doors and were herded down to the Queens Vaults where it was felt they would be safe. This wasn't such a good idea as a mob of Docks boys came out of the side-street and caved in the windows before being chased off by police. Next late-comers from Bristol were bombarded with glasses and bottles as they passed a nearby pub while being escorted to the Queens Vaults. A girl that works in the pub said that the Worzels were demanding they be allowed to walk unescorted to Ninian Park and a Chief Copper had called their bluff and said, "Ok then, off you go." They changed their minds and decided they needed an escort. I was stood outside the club shop when two Worzels were brought in a cop van, one with blood all over his head and obviously in shock, to be handed over to the St John's Ambulance crew. After the game hundreds of Cardiff rioted in an attempt to get at the Worzels but were beaten back by the Old Bill. You can see from this picture, the railings were torn out of the ground as the mob charged across the field and bricked the coaches. You've got to give it to the

Worzels, both Bristol City and Bristol Rovers, they are usually game and always try to have it with Cardiff. In Bristol mind you, both teams have a habit of picking off small groups returning to cars and don't mind hitting scarfers, so be careful if travelling there.

Stoke away

A few years ago the Castle Pub took a coach to Stoke. The coaches all stopped in Stafford and Cardiff absolutely wrecked the place. The police forced all the boys onto trains and took them to Stoke where local buses had been laid on to take the boys to the ground. Cardiff decided they would rather walk in the sunshine and kicked all the bus windows out and ended up being walked to the ground. Cardiff's firm arrived halfway through the match and proceeded to riot in the ground. After the match in the car park, Stoke are up above us raining bricks down and loads of Cardiff are being hit by stones. The police don't care and are too busy hitting Cardiff boys to stop the stone-throwers. This is too much for the Cardiff and they rip down one fence and run for the second which is all that separates the two mobs. The first fence went down and Nicky L is trapped under it and everyone's running across it. The Cardiff can't get over the second fence as there's loads of police

Cardiff fans in violent flare-up

POLICE were today studying CCTV footage after violence flared during yesterday's Stoke City 2-1 win over Cardiff City when supporters tore down security fences and threw coins and missiles from the stands.

The game was the subject of a heavy police presence following threats of violence posted on the Internet by rival fans.

Staffordshire police said it deployed 600 officers and made 20 arrests before kick-off, mostly for alcohol-related offences.

A police spokesman said searches of travelling fans' coaches and at the Britannia Stadium turned up various potential weapons, including a circular saw and 100 Stanley knife blades.

During the match, Stoke boosted their chances of a Second Division play-off place as they overcame their relegation-threatened rivals in front of 14,000 spectators.

About 2,000 Cardiff fans were expected to travel to the Potteries for the fixture, but police had warned anyone without a ticket to stay away.

A search area was set up at the ground to stop troublemakers bringing in weapons, and the empty section of seating between rival fans was widened and filled with several layers of security fencing.

At one stage during the match, the police presence prevented Cardiff's Andy Legg from taking a corner as mounted police officers were in the way.

During play, several seats were ripped up and coins and drink were thrown at police.

A police spokesman said the police operation had been "a tremendous success", adding: "The intention was to, when it occurred to resolve it effectively, with the minimum use of force and the minimum number of injuries."

battling with them to stop it. One of Stoke's top boys told me that the talk amongst the Stoke was that if the last fence had gone, they don't know whether they could have stood as Cardiff were so mental and there were too many.

In the middle of all this mayhem if you watch the video, you can see all sorts of bricks bouncing off a yellow Thomas Motors of Barry coach. Luckily the windows didn't go in. All in all a good laugh although due to CCTV everyone involved was arrested in a massive operation and some big jail was had. Brick got away with it as he had suffered from 'Stoke Flu' and wouldn't get out of bed in the morning to catch the coach. This is the game that ended up with Operation Javelin and loads of arrests of both sides."

Stoke City v Cardiff City 2002

After the rioting at the notorious fixture between these two clubs in 2000, police mounted one of the largest operations in the history of the domestic game. Staffordshire police, a small force of just 2,000 officers, called on other forces to turn out a thousand officers on the day. The game was stopped for seven minutes as the police attempted to arrest Stoke hooligans in the ground. After the game police were pelted with stones. Cardiff owner Sam Hamamm returned to his car to find it was vandalised by Stoke lads.

Funny story 2003 - Ex-soccer minder admits hoax

"...A former minder of Cardiff City Football Club owner Sam Hammam has admitted setting off a fire alarm in the hotel where a rival team was sleeping before a crucial match. Neil M, 39, set off a fire alarm at the Celtic Manor Resort, Newport, in the early hours of 25 May. Queens Park Rangers players were staying at the hotel before their Division Two play-off final against Cardiff at the Millennium Stadium later that day. M pleaded guilty to causing criminal damage and giving a false fire alarm. But he denied the offence was football-related in the hearing at Newport Magistrates Court. Paul Moore prosecuting, said, "There will be legal argument as to whether the offence was football-related. It will be the prosecution's suggestion that this was football-related and we will invite a banning order. This will be opposed by the defence."

He was released on unconditional bail to reappear at the court on 16th July when another hearing will decide whether the hoax was aimed at the QPR players. Some 200 people had to leave the Celtic Manor while the alarm was investigated. The QPR players were able to stay inside as they were sleeping in a different wing of the hotel. The alarm went off at 3:00am, 12 hours before QPR's play-off final kicked off at Cardiff's Millennium Stadium which the London team lost 1-0 in extra time. Shame.

Hull

Hull undoubtedly have a lot of lads. Some Cardiff rate them highly, others don't. The time they came to Cardiff on a Friday night, they had a good 100 lads. They left the ground and while most of the Cardiff were trying to get out, they went for a bit of handbags in the car park, waving arms about. A few stones were thrown and they were put back on their coaches before any proper Cardiff were even out of the ground. They went on to gloat about it on the net which made them look a bit stupid to say the least.

Hull had a major result down in Swansea when they apparently managed to get there undetected by the Old Bill, entered the Garibaldi, Swansea's boozer and smashed the windows. Now Swansea can usually raise a nasty bunch down there so this took bottle. Seems they got away with it as Swansea were totally unprepared and didn't expect it. Respect to them for this. If the Jacks had all their boys there, they could have taken a serious hiding and they didn't know what the Jacks had there.

Huddersfield away by A

"I remember going to Huddersfield with a full mob of proper boys who I'd be happy to go with anywhere. We stopped off at Manchester for a few beers and a look around. About twelve of us decided not to go back on the coach and instead get the train to the stop before Huddersfield. We all get off at Stalybridge and make our way to the nearest pub. A few of us go in this pub which weren't that much different from the shitholes in Barry. A few went into this wine bar up the road. When the lads in the pub arrived at the wine bar to meet the rest, it became a bit lively and we were politely asked to vacate the premises! So we rung a taxi firm and asked for a mini-bus to take us to Huddersfield. The mini bus turns up and we're all thinking right ten minutes and we'll be there. About three quarters of an hour later after travelling through the last of the summer wine country, we arrived. We stepped off the mini-bus and walked through the town centre. As we approached McDonalds, we saw a small mob of boys take off up a side street. A few excited lads took off after them picking up the obligatory milk/beer bottles on the way to present to them but they were gone like greased lightning.

We carried on through the town centre and were eventually found by the Old Bill who held our hands to the pub just outside the stadium where the Huddersfield usually go. There were hundreds of Cardiff there, a fucking impressive mob if I ever saw one. As the start of the game approached, a few of us thought we would nip off and have a few beers elsewhere. We found this little pub not far away and settled down for a few pints and a chat with Uncle Charles. We were refreshed after a few and decided to go to the game but not in the Cardiff end! We went in singles and the guys on the turnstile must of thought we were fucking mad (we were!). Anyway they just let us in and we made our way to the seats. After about two minutes of getting in and sitting down Leo Fortune West scored. We all looked at each other for a split second and then went mad, jumping up and down and singing

KAAARDIFF like we were on our own end!

Well that didn't go down to well and a few Northern chappies let us know how they felt about us. The stewards were there like a shot and we decided to make our own way out, letting them who were waiting for burgers, etc know who we were but no-one wanted to play just call us names from a distance. We reached the bottom of the stairs and the stewards didn't have a clue. They chucked a few out of the gate but me and Monster ducked off and saw one steward, looking after the gate which led to the side of the pitch, skinny as fuck and as wet as a used condom he was! We told him that the other steward had told us to go this way and just walked past him, straight alongside the pitch as the game was going on. The two of us laughing like fuck at the silly cunts sat in the stand who were chucking stuff at us. The stewards didn't know how the fuck we got there only realizing when we reached the away end. They called the Old Bill over and we were escorted into the away end to rapturous applause from the Cardiff who had seen us from where they were.

There were two little mobs of us in the home end and this went down well with the lads who were in the away end. Respect to both mobs (you know who you are). Just before the end of the game, we had all grouped up and left the stadium and made our way to the car park. We all met up in the car park and waited for Huddersfield to come out. We were all waiting by the coaches when we heard a few Dingle voices giving it the usual mouth. I chased one up the bank but he was gone through the bushes head first! I went back to where the boys were and found out that one of the boys was missing a tooth due to being sucker punched by some cunt who smacked him and legged it! Then about 20-30 of them appeared and I thought this is it, we're off and steamed in thinking that all the rest were behind me. As I reached them and started having it with one of them, an Old Bill came out the darkness and whacked me right in the mooey with his baton and tried gripping me. I squirmed away and returned to the boys and was told that I was on my own when I steamed them. The rest of the boys had spotted the Old Bill and thought fuck that! Lucky as fuck that I was never nicked and I never even cared about the cap I lost getting away from them! The toothless one managed to keep his tooth and put it in his pocket only to realise when we returned to Barry that he lost it on the journey home! The funniest part of the day was seeing one of the lads being given a backy on the back of a BMX off some chavvy kid to the pub we were in."

Southampton Away
This is the view from some Southampton boys
"Cardiff had a bunch better than anything I have ever seen at Southampton to be

fair. They would have shat anyone. All this 'where else could anyone waited around for pubs to let them in' shit is gay. Reading away this season for one Southampton were all over the town. But good luck to the filthy non-English freaks, they seem to shit up coppers."

"Apparently Cardiff had 100 odd that did 30 saints in St Mary's Road as well as a few of their herberts causing a few problems up Bedford place. Possibly a few isolated rows but that's what I was told."

"I took a wrong turning after game and walked the wrong way for half hour. When I returned to the top of the hill looking down at the station, I noticed a few likely looking lads across the road opposite KFC. I went across to have a look. There was about 10 Southampton and one of them was almost crying with cuts under each eye. He told the Old Bill that a Cardiff fan had banged him a couple of times. These 10 were all dressers but were still giving Old Bill descriptions. In actual fact, Cardiff overran the town and caused havoc everywhere. The Southampton seemed to want to try and have goes in small groups and were getting demolished. Very disappointing but what do you expect?"

In 2003, a 56 year old man was savagely beaten in **Port Talbot** while trying to defend his 17 year old son from an attack by two men. They had attacked his son who was wearing a Swansea City shirt after shouting 'Cardiff City' at him near the town's market. The 56 year old was admitted to Morriston Hospital with serious head injuries thus proving that Cardiff have their bullies too.

Two quote: by Chelsea Grass Darren Wells on BBC Hooligans Programme.
'Everyone who knows Cardiff knows Simmo'
'Everyone who goes to Cardiff is a bit wary, coz of the numbers they've got'.

You'll never ban a City fan
A football thug has had a banning order extended to 2013 after he went to a Cardiff City home game. Colin C, 40, of Barry, was originally banned from watching any matches for six years in 2002. He was hit with the original order after getting caught up in violent scenes during the Bluebirds' famous FA Cup win against Leeds United as well as being jailed for 75 days for his part in the trouble.

But after being released, he was again jailed for four years in April, 2004, after driving a van into the front of Fairwater Police Station which demolished the entrance doors, brought down a ceiling and left the civilian clerk in shock. The court was told he smashed into the building and shouted to chasing officers, "I did it for the Soul Crew." But his latest refusal to comply with the ban means the Dad of three now has to stay away from football grounds for a further five years. He was seen at Ninian Park during this season's home game against Wolverhampton Wanderers.

David Collins, author of 'Born under a Grange End Star'.
"I have seen large bricks hurled into piles of Burnley fans, hand to hand combat at Fulham, piles of debris thrown at Swansea players at the Vetch, bottles thrown at Roger Freestone during a testimonial, heard ugly chants about the Yorkshire Ripper or opposing fans that have committed suicide and seen Argentinian flags displayed at home games against English teams. A two pronged pitch invasion at Luton had to be seen to be believed. I heard rumours that CS gas was used. At a Wales International at Ninian Park in 1976, someone even threw a corner flag at a linesman."

In recent years Cardiff have played some high profile teams like Tottenham away where the trouble was so bad it was described as 'like the 70's' with large groups of blacks attacking a pub full of Cardiff scarfers and smashing all the windows with baseball bats while kids screamed and hid under tables. It kicked off everywhere all day and was extremely nasty with several Cardiff being tooled by Tottenham.

West Ham came to Cardiff and a dedicated group of Soul Crew attacked the escort with bricks and bottles and some of them were banned for five years and some jailed for four years. At West Ham away, there was trouble too.

Here's **Kane of the ICF's** story.
"Well you lot showed in numbers and seeing as you lot come on coaches, it did take us a bit by surprise. We were expecting a good mob but nothing like the size of the mob you did bring. Before the game, neither side could really get anywhere near each other due to the complete Old Bill overkill that we have all come to expect these days. After the game a few of us slipped off early, only to get rounded up and strip searched in the back of a meat wagon. Once released, we waited down the Barking road as you lot had been kept behind. A few of our mates were waiting down by the East Ham social club when a good mob of your lot, about 30-40, arrived and ran us down the road where we regrouped. Then your mob that were already on coaches saw what was happening and a few got off and gave West Ham a slap. Down on the Barking Road however, we still had good numbers of about 75-100 main lads. We dished out a few slaps and a few lads got a tug. Then the Old Bill took control and

split up everyone. You lot were taken down the Barking Road towards East Ham where the majority of lads were locked in pubs and unable to get out. A few did manage to get out though and threw bottles, etc at the coaches but nothing major.

You're the only team to bring a mob to West Ham since the early 90's and fair play to you, you probably had the better of us that day. Cardiff gained a lot of respect that day."

Coventry Away news report from South Wales Echo

RIVAL soccer gangs used the internet to plan a mass fight in Coventry city centre. They first used message boards to taunt each other and then set the venue for the violent ruck by mobile phone. A Sky Blues fan named in court as 'Big Kev' fixed the site for the pitch battle with Cardiff City supporters. Unfortunately for the fighters, he chose a place well-covered by CCTV cameras and police from South Wales used the images to track down seven Cardiff culprits. The extraordinary events leading to the 'scrap of the day' were told to Coventry Crown Court yesterday when two of the thugs were sentenced. This led to a good few of Cardiff's boys being banned or jailed too. All this has had a big effect on the firm.

Hull away 2005 -2006 season by Mike

"Hull were getting a bit of a reputation as a tidy firm although I had seen no evidence of this. Some of our older lads however insisted that they can turn out a tidy mob at home. I suppose any Northern shithole that's actually a city can turn out decent numbers. I jumped on the Rams coach and off we went. We stopped at a nearby town and a good 300-400 of us made our way to get the train to Hull. As usual these days, the Old Bill fucked it up for us and after much scuffling, we were forced back onto our coaches. In the ground the Cardiff boys grabbed a steward and tried to get his keys off him to open the gates so we could get at Hull but the old bastard struggled like mad and escaped. I could not bring myself to chin him as he was too old so we gave up that plan and charged outside into the car park. We had 600 lads and were well pissed off as Cardiff had lost 2-0. The game had now finished and the Hull were streaming out into the car park. We started ripping down the fence to get at them. The fence was barely holding up as mounted police battered us and we battled with them in our desperate struggle to get at our rivals. The Old Bill and Cardiff were both taking some serious casualties as the battle waged on for about 20 minutes. Despite this, the Hull boys made no attempt to have a go back and were content to just throw stones from a safe distance. I wasn't impressed with them and think they are seriously overrated.

No disrespect to Hull as I know they are a good mob on their day. Seems they've gone downhill these days mind but it's probably due to police crackdowns and CCTV. Same as at Cardiff. You can't expect people to keep putting their jobs, relationships and freedom on the line with such a high chance of getting caught. The last time Cardiff arranged to go up there for an organised 'off', two coaches of boys turned up in Cardiff to get the buses to Hull only to find the Old Bill had cancelled the coaches. I hear this has also happened in Hull where they have had coaches cancelled at the last minute too. The police have it all wrapped up these days."

Wolves v Cardiff 2006 by C Squad

"Another game with great potential to kick off. Five of us, four of which were older lads, travelled in a van and arrived in Wolverhampton around 2:00pm. We parked the van and using our best Brummy accents blagged our way into a home pub. We had a pint and set off to the ground. As we approached the ground, a few likely looking Wolves were standing by a burger van. I went over and started chatting with them and telling them that we were getting kept in after the game. We were spotted by Cardiff's Old Bill and taken into the ground. From a distance, we saw a huge escort of lads walking towards us which turned out to be Cardiff. We entered the ground and headed for our seats.

Half time came and most lads went for a drink under the stands. The bar staff refused to serve anyone and in a matter of seconds a chant of 'We want beer!' went up and the shutters were nearly ripped off. The Old Bill steamed into the crowd of Cardiff, making space between us and the bar. They started lashing out with their batons and shields so everyone piled in, giving as good as they got. I tried explaining to a Cardiff steward that all we wanted was a pint and that if we were served, none of this would have happened. We were then forced into the seating area where one copper took it upon himself to put me on my arse and strike me whilst down. I was fuming and had to be calmed by a few lads in the seats.

The five of us on the van decided to leave early and made our way back to the van. All the way home, I received calls saying it was going off with the Old Bill outside and that the Wolves made few attempts to attack the escort. The thing that made my day, was when I was told a copper was KO'ed by a bin and a cheeky slag Old Bill was put on her fat arse."

Wolves have always had a good mob especially at home and I was well impressed with their numbers in the 80's when I went there. These days however, although they still have a lot of boys, trips there are usually 'bubbles'. West Midlands Police are bastards and will literally nick you for anything. A lot of our boys don't bother going there these days.

Bristol City kicked off in the Grange end recently. The Old Bill steamed into them and one copper ended up with a broken arm and another with a broken ankle. Fair play to them but madness because when they get nicked, they'll get some jail for that.

Dutch firm FC Twente

These guys caught Cardiff on the hop. They arrived early, a good 100 and they had twenty Chelsea boys with them too. Cardiff desperately scrambled around for a mob to confront them and it ended up with them trashing Dempsey's bar and 15 hardcore Soul Crew battling with them in the Brewery Quarter and apparently running them after an exchange of plastic chairs. The Chelsea group were fronted by around the same number and were asked to go somewhere away from the cameras but replied, "We've only come for a nose, we don't wanna know." In typical style of 'today's hooligans', they (the Dutch) went off and talked a load of shite about it on the internet, how they battered Cardiff, etc. The fact is, if anyone had expected them to come as a firm, they would have been destroyed.

Here's NT from Ystrad's story

After coming back from a long ban and visiting Old Trafford, Leeds, Reading, Spurs and even England passing without major incident, I'd decided the casual lark was over for me. But this day, I had a call at 12:30pm telling me that there was a mob of Dutch roaming the city centre. Now rumours like this have become almost tradition down the City and for most games it is usually a firm of ghost as very few firms venture to Cardiff with the intention of confrontation. But this call came from an old friend whose info was always spot on and he'd actually set eyes on them. At the time I was so uninterested that I did not even know we were playing anyone. However, as usual, the mere mention of a firm in Cardiff got the bug we just can't get rid of going again so I thought I'd slide into town for a look after work.

I arrived in Cardiff around 5ish passing Edwards where a few of the Merthyr lot were humouring football intelligence. I quickly said my 'hello's and goodbyes' in the same breath and headed for Sam's Bar to meet up with a few of the lads. I inquired if there'd been any action. As usual, all was quiet but apparently the Dutch were still in Cardiff so we settled outside Sam's bar. There was around 20 City milling about among the Saturday night revellers. Football intelligence soon planted up and proceeded to film us for the next few hours. This was why I became fed up with following City so we decided to give them the slip and meet up further along the road in the Hard Rock Café where we continued to carry on with the night until someone mentioned there was a mob of FC Twente out the back.

Again, that bug kicked in. Too much temptation not to have a nose so me and Will had a quick waltz through them. Being only 5' 7", I was fed up of making eye contact with their chests to be honest. The most interesting thing was to catch a few cockney accents in amongst them. Now this was confusing so we headed for the balcony to get a better vantage point. On surveying them, they had a good 30+ but there seemed to be different faces coming and going all the time. There was also groups of Valley lads in amongst them. With Cardiff having such a catchment area, you are never going to know every lad who likes his nonsense but I never set eyes on any of these during any previous years down the City so I wasn't all that confident in our front line at this stage.

A few lads from Bridgend joined us and we talked quietly between ourselves as our numbers grew to about the same. We watched as heated chats were going on between both sets including two Chelsea lads who were putting on a show for their Dutch hosts. Most lads don't want to chat in this situation or are too clueless to spot the danger but this was only going to end in one way. This is the time that takes an age. You know it's going to happen. You just didn't know when and all this was going on as the place filled with party goers oblivious to what was about to happen.

Obviously, before the days of CCTV, you could just wade in and take your chances. However football intelligence was already on to us and one of ours had already been told outside the Yard to do himself a favour and leave. Frankly looking round I didn't fancy our chances as this Dutch lot dwarfed most of us and I wasn't the only one. Boys I had known for years came and went just as quick. Whether they were on a promise or had had a long enough day already or didn't fancy the odds or what, I won't judge but this was just about to go up in the air. Then that unmistakable sound went up. In a split second, I realised my hunch about our front line talkers was spot on as most quickly retreated, passing us and ducking for cover. It was our little band of merry men who were in the thick of it. Luckily the small group of lads were more than willing to step in. A flurry of punches and kicks were thrown as a few dropped from both sides. Both firms backed off. Glasses, chairs, tables, signs and anything that could be thrown was then hurled back and forth as the chant of 'Soul Crew' and whatever they were bellowing filled the air.

Then the famous 'no mans land' appeared. This is where it's men from the boys time. A few of us walked forward. Me with my arms firmly by my side, only raising them to deflect the odd bottle or chair seeing as arm waving things become a criminal offence these days. It was their turn to make a stand. A few of their stragglers were booted up the arse as they backed off. We stood waiting for them to charge back into us but once they'd used up all their missiles, they were on their toes. If ever the Soul Crew name and reputation was evident, this was such an occasion. When I turned around, although numbers were even to start with, I realised there was only about 15 of us who'd actually gone into them. The lads from my way who I could always rely on Will, Pricey and Curpy and a mixture of lads from Bridgend, Caerphilly and two brothers from Cardiff and their mates joined us.

This was nowhere near the Soul Crew's finest but goes to show a bit of bottle will see you ok when it comes on top and gets you a result when odds are stacked. Respect to all those there that night. Soon after the Old Bill had waded in and shut down the area. We were on our toes but still clocked the amount of Joe publics who'd had their mobiles out filming the incident. I've read many articles how the public had been left terrified by football casuals over the years but this crowd seemed amused and excited by what they'd just witnessed. I think there was only one bird crying and if I am honest, looking at her I bet that was a regular occurrence when attention was deflected from her.

On reaching St Mary's Street, we ran into the cockney translator who was having his head bandaged up by Paramedics. I couldn't resist tapping him on the back to advise him he'd best come to Cardiff with Chelsea instead next time.

Now it was paranoia time. Surely it was on camera. This is the bit we all hate but a quick ring around a few doormen and word was there was no video evidence result. Rumours soon went around the net that the Dutch had smashed us... the cheek! This was put to rest recently when a few lads run into a few of their's in a pre-season tour of Portugal where they admitted they came off second best.

When **Tottenham's 'Yid Army'** came to Cardiff recently, a Cardiff Under 5 fired a flare into the away end resulting in a ten year ban for him but some good footage on Youtube. They marched to and from the ground with a good 200 lads, massive police escort, giving it the 'big 'un', however as they passed the Grange pub where a lot of the old Cardiff heads were shouting abuse at them, they made no effort to break the escort at all to have a go. Seems to me they were happy to stay in their escort, safe as houses, then go home saying how shit Cardiff were like a lot of them do these days. They would never have done this back in the day before the Old Bill had it sewn up. A few Cardiff jumped out of a van and tried to attack the escort but were arrested and banned for five years. Later, some older Cardiff lads bumped into some Yids in a chippie and absolutely battered them although I doubt they'd ever admit it.

Barnsley brought a good firm of around 120 to Cardiff recently and a few scuffles went off firstly in St Mary Street but the Old Bill had it mostly sewn up. I have been told by some boys that they had a good go here and were well game. They were taken to the Philharmonic pub by the Police and escaped out the fire exits. In the lane at the back, they found themselves confronted by Cardiff's finest including the Docks lot. They stood and had a good go but were demolished. At the end of the game, they attempted to get out into the street where a large mob of Cardiff were pelting them with stones and bottles but they were battered back in by the police. There is good footage of this scrap going around which shows the police knocking

Soccer thugs clash before City game

VIOLENCE flared ahead of Cardiff City's game with Barnsley on Saturday.

Riot police and mounted officers had to deal with drunken brawling fans near Sam's Bar and Walkabout on St Mary Street.

Three men were arrested, a 26-year-old from Cardiff for violent disorder and a 35-year-old man also from the city for a public order offence.

A 33-year-old from Barnsley was arrested in connection with a drugs offence.

There was trouble between rival supporters at a number of bars in St Mary Street and police said one bar was left badly damaged.

At one point Barnsley fans tried to break out of the ground's visitors' section, but police using batons kept them at bay.

There were no further arrests for violence, but a Cardiff man was arrested for a drugs offence.

Police said there were no reports of violence after the game.

Supt Kevin Tumelty said: "The majority of games this season have passed without incident and it's disappointing that a small number of hooligans, from both Cardiff and Barnsley, were openly seeking confrontation with each other."

● Match report, see Monday Sport

out several of them and dishing out serious violence to the Barnsley fans. I almost felt sorry for them (not). Respect to them for turning up though and having a go. **Valley Boy** says **Barnsley** had such a good turnout at Cardiff apparently because they were commemorating the death of one of their lads. Like many before them however, they bumped into the wrong Cardiff lot (Docks etc) and took a bad slapping.

Ajax
These Dutch morons headed for Cardiff as a lot of mobs do these days knowing

that the Police will be in 'overkill mode' and they won't really be in any danger. For weeks before the game, they were on the internet shouting about how they were going to do the famous Soul Crew, etc. As it happens, their escort of around 100 'lads' (tramps) was escorted by about three times as many police. In the ground, they threw seats and made a big fuss and a few were arrested. One of the muppets was nicked for attempting to streak!!! At the end of the game, they all ran outside and minor disorder occurred with a large number of YOUNG Cardiff kids.

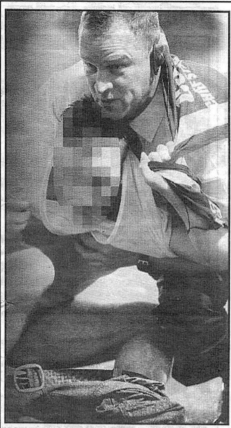

PROBLEMS: A steward holds on to a man who tried to streak across the pitch   PICTURE: Wales News

Seven held after City and Ajax clashes

POLICE made seven arrests in total relating to Cardiff City's clash with Ajax.

A police spokeswoman said: "South Wales Police football officers, in conjunction with Dutch police, based the policing plan for the Cardiff v Ajax match on intelligence that suggested a significant number of Dutch "risk" supporters were travelling to the game at Ninian Park."

Police estimate that 400 to 600 Dutch fans were in the city in the run-up to the match. There were a number of incidents throughout the day involving criminal damage and low level public order. The majority of fans were well behaved, however a small number of Ajax and Cardiff fans did become involved in disorder during the match and later in St Mary Street. There were seven arrests in total for low level public order and one for invading the pitch.

"South Wales Police implement plans for matches on a case by case basis – based on intelligence. There is no intelligence to suggest any significant problems at the first game of the season next Saturday – however there will be sufficient police officers on duty to deal with any disorder that should arise."

As they were escorted through Riverside, they were scuffling with the police and a large number of knives were found that they had dropped. Later a group of about ten attacked four Cardiff lads in a Spar and although one Cardiff lad ended up with a broken arm and another was stabbed in the chest with a sharpened umbrella, on good authority the Dutch then received a serious slapping from the Cardiff boys.

They resorted to throwing tins of beans, etc at the Cardiff lads until the police came to rescue them. Later a small group of Cardiff attacked their hotel in the Roath area. They took a few digs and refused to come out. The Echo reported seven arrests with minor incidents breaking out here, there and everywhere but no massive row as would have happened in the past before the Old Bill set to work smashing Cardiff's mob.

This writer on a Cardiff message board backs up this here:
To argue my case, we witness around 120 Ajax casuals marched into the Grange End around 7:35pm on Friday. They were kept in a 'safe pub' in town and given Old Bill escort to and from the city centre. However despite the odd rumour of a slap here and there, there was no real disorder from the City lads towards Ajax, just great banter in the stadium as it should be, helping to create a great atmosphere. No mobs of lads picking them off on Sloper Rd, no welcoming committee of 400 lads outside the away end prior to the game, no organised mob of 200 challenging them drinking in our bars before the game, etc....

Now the point here is in the mid 90's, all of the above would have happened and did indeed happen on a regular basis. Remember Plymouth, Boro, Barnsley, Rovers, even carnage after Liege home in the Cup Winners cup with crowds of 6,000 !!!! There was always a sizeable hardcore in town waiting for fans to come and then 'ave a go at them'.

Thankfully since Operation Javelin, I think it was after the Stoke game and large numbers being lifted, effectively the Soul Crew are no longer the force they once were. Yes, granted there are still lads in Block A and Grange and we can organise a mob of chav looking hooligans to some degree even in 2008 but the point is, nothing like the mid 90's. The hooligans are definitely being eradicated.

I think we can agree the numpties are on their way out as a whole and the Ajax game confirms this whereby an organised mob of casuals from Holland were looking for trouble but they were not met by an organised response as they would have been a few years ago. The Echo, bans and CCTV have put paid to the way of life for hundreds of people!

This guy is absolutely spot on. The Soul Crew have been largely crippled by the authorities which now allows mugs like these to come and in their words 'take the piss'.

As predicted they then went online and said 'Soul Crew mugs', 'where are your Soul Crew?', etc. This is typical of today's 'Hooligan', especially the Dutch who in my opinion are showing a pattern here. With both FC Twente and Ajax and at Wales games, after throwing things, they seemed reluctant to get into major fisticuffs and usually run when they have nothing left to throw and for this reason, I feel they lack bottle and are mostly 'wannabees'. They'll never match up to British Hooligans, end of chat.

A Damaged Firm?

Quite obviously Ninian Park has been one of the worst places ever for opposing fans since the 70's. Nowadays however, due to banning orders, CCTV, harassment of lads, it seems to have died a death at Cardiff. At a recent game against Hull, I was standing outside hoping to get photos of trouble and I witnessed about 100 Cardiff kids and I mean KIDS having running battles with the police. These guys were aged between about 14-16 and have obviously seen the Football Factory and want to get involved. The Hull lads must have thought it was hilarious to see this 'kiddy firm' giving it large.

You have to respect these kids for having a pop mind. It's not their fault they were born too late to have a glittering career as hooligans but they really are wasting their time. You can't get away with anything these days. Back before CCTV and when the police weren't clued up, you could get away with anything. I know lads who were hooligans at the City for years, never were caught and are now high ranking police officers or Solicitors. These days you wouldn't last two minutes before you were behind bars and they can arrest you months or even years later. Any visitors to Cardiff these days must surely realise the glory days of the mad Cardiff mob are all but over. Or are they?

The main faces are still around. It's just that life has been made very difficult for a lot of them. They are what's known as 'sleeping supporters'. They can suddenly re-appear at certain games where a massive mob seems to appear from nowhere. Like at Millwall '99. You'll never TRULY ban a City fan. Watch this space.

Further reading :

'Soul Crew' by Tony Rivers and Dave Jones (Milo Books)
'Diary of the Real Soul Crew' by Annis Abraham (Headhunter Books)

Chapter Ten
Maesteg and the KKK

In the late 80's, Allan Beshella, a former 'Grand Wizard' of the Ku Klux Klan, moved to Maesteg from his home in California and with him came a load of trouble. Local (non football) Skinheads flocked round him and he began to hold noisy parties at his home with 50-100 Skinheads from all over Wales in attendance, all Seig Heiling to racist bands like Skrewdriver in his back garden. It was one of these parties which launched him to notoriety.

K takes up the story
"As the party raged on and an effigy of a black man was burned, a few cars of Anti Racist Campaigners pulled up. Needless to say, 30 seconds after getting out their loudspeakers, they were surrounded by Skinheads and kicked to fuck. One guy was almost kicked to death and several boys received jail sentences for this attack.

This started a long war between Beshella and his cronies and various left wing groups which went on for a large part of the 90's. Several times anti-Racists went to his house and smashed windows or trashed his car. They even tried to poison his two pet Dobermans. Within months of him moving to Wales, racial conflict in the area was rife. Hate mail to Asians, battles with Reds (Communists), KKK graffiti all over Maesteg and a massive rise in reported racial incidents. Then the shit really hit the fan. The Jewish graves in Ely Cemetery were spray painted with Swastikas. This caused absolute murder. Marches, battles, media smear campaigns, police raids, the lot.

Among all the boys we were hanging around with at the time, I swear that none of us knew who had done this. My theory is that it was either the police or the Reds. It did the white racist groups no favours at all and just made the ordinary man in the street see us as nutters which we wanted to avoid at all costs. I was a member of the BNP at the time and as the first Candidate had been voted in at the Isle of Dogs, we really thought we were on our way to electoral success. The BNP wanted to leave the Skinhead image behind and present themselves as respectable, which clearly they are not. It has to be said that the Skinheads surrounding Beshella at the time were nothing whatsoever to do with football violence. They were all political or music Skins. Although there were a few small groups amongst the Soul Crew that were racist, attempts to recruit them often failed as they are unwilling to do the mundane things like leafleting and many of them were into drugs which conflicts with the Nazi ideals. Believe it or not, the really bad Nazis are very anti-drug. They see it as a scum thing for Reds and students to pickle their brains with. On occasion some Skins would go to Cardiff games and plant stickers around the grounds but as I say, attempts to politicise Cardiff's Hooligan Firm turned out to be a waste of time."

Child Sex Offender?

Beshella's house was put under 24 hour surveillance by the police and Security Services as the Media went into overdrive. They announced that he had a conviction for a child sex offence in 1972 in California. Although he denied this and blamed it on a smear campaign, a few of his supporters walked away from him after this. It has to be said that all the racist Skins were here long before Beshella arrived. He just served as a focal point for a set of circumstances to evolve, made much worse by the involvement of Anti-Racist Campaigners. Combat 18 head man, Charlie Sargent was a regular visitor who flooded South Wales with C18 and White Wolves literature. He instigated a riot in Caerphilly where an anti-racist meeting in a pub was attacked and many arrests followed.

The **Anti-Nazi League** led by a Peter Jackson and made up mostly of left-wing students, gays and lesbians (but hardly any immigrants) launched a Cardiff based war on racists which involved protesting outside the houses of anyone they felt was racist including a Doctor who had prepared a report pointing out certain racial differences affecting treatments. They also sent threatening mail to anyone they felt wasn't helping them in their war on racism.

Back to K's story

"A massive anti-racist march was organised in Cardiff and a good few thousand of the great unwashed turned up and marched through the streets chanting on loudspeakers and bullying watchers into signing a petition to end racism. At Roath, they were attacked by a certain long haired racist and his gang who broke one guy's jaw and stole a petition he was carrying. They then visited all the people who had signed it at night and damaged their houses/cars.

Next someone started sending out flyers stating that the BNP was holding public meetings in various towns round South Wales. This was a hoax - the BNP knew nothing about the meetings. However, when the media contacted the BNP, they would refuse to comment and so the media believed it to be true."

The Penrhys Meeting

K Says: "At the time we didn't know who was organizing the meetings but we read in the Echo that a meeting was organised at Penrhys, one of the roughest estates in South Wales. To give you an idea of how rough it is, I'll tell you the story of when they were trying to build new houses up there. Every time the builders put materials there, it was stolen. Bricks, sand, you name it. As soon as it arrived, they would steal it. So the builders employed a security firm to guard the site. The locals beat up the two security guards and locked them in a metal container while they robbed the site. The only way the builders could finish the job was to pay the local hard men to guard the site. That's how rough the place is. They even torched the police station up there once.

So anyway, on the day, we turned up at the Square in Penrhys and there's around 100 locals and about 20 Reds. We had thought about parking in the main car-park but as there were several cars up on blocks, we went further down the mountain and parked, then walked up. Some Homo walks up to me and tries to give us leaflets. I slapped them out of his hands. Next thing, we're in a massive argument with all these Reds and all these nasty locals come over and start mouthing. I told him we aren't Nazis, just Welsh boys looking to protect our heritage. He's not having any of it and insists on calling us Nazis. There are four coppers on the road below, seemingly uninterested in the situation developing around them. Some nasty looking guy comes up and says,

"What have you got a knife for?"
"I haven't got a knife you clown," I said.
"Why are your mates tooled up then?" he replied.
"Ask them," I said. So he turns to J who's a mental case and says
"Why have you got a knife?"
"To cut you up you cunt," J replies. He turns to his mates and says, "Go and get the tools."

As this little weasel runs off, I asked the boys if they thought we should fuck off sharpish. They all agreed it would be wise. We walked away and just as we were passing the police, a roar went up and about 20 of them came around the corner carrying Samurai swords, hammers and even a ball and chain. We broke into a sprint and one of our boys goes arse over head and ripped all his leg open on the concrete. As he stood up a copper said, "That'll teach you, you cunt." Charming!

As we ran down the mountain, we heard them shouting to cut us off at the car park. If we had been parked there, we would have been dead. This was a close escape and I still have nightmares about it."

The Pontypridd meeting
Another meeting was arranged in Ponty. About 100 protesters turned up and attacked a pub where some Skinheads were drinking and then rampaged through the town centre until four of them were arrested for fighting with the police. When they went to Ponty magistrates, the Judge allowed them to remain anonymous for fear of reprisals, something which is unheard of in the Courts such was the fear of these people. When Romper Stomper was shown in Ponty, the anti-racist protesters were attacked with CS gas and several of them were put in hospital.

K takes up the story again
"It was around this time that Pete Jackson and his cronies made a fatal error. They started to mouth off about a lot of the racist attacks being done by the Soul Crew. This was quite clearly bollocks but it got a lot of the footie boys' backs up. The ANL then became a target for some Casuals who previously wouldn't have been interested in them. A few of them were battered while leafleting in Ely by football lads, then Pete Jackson and a bird were kicked unconscious in Barry town centre by Under 5s, (Young Hooligans). That was the last time he was ever heard of. Not long after this, Beshella and his main boys were targeted and loads of raids happened which effectively put them out of business. He was then jailed for abusing a shopkeeper and I walked away from it all as I'm not into the Nazi thing. I was fed up of having it forced down my neck by the BNP. Those days in the early 90's were mad but it couldn't go on as racists are seen as worse than paedophiles by the authorities.

In my opinion, since 9/11 there's no point being a racial agitator - the Muslims are doing a good enough job of making people hate them on their own. I'll let them get on with it."

Sargent was also convicted of stabbing another right wing activist to death and at the trial it came out that he had been working for MI5 so while he was encouraging the South Wales Skinheads to attack immigrants and lefties, he was secretly grassing them up which led to their demise. He's now serving life for the murder and the far right seems to have died a death in Wales apart from in Jackland. Cardiff's football mob have had three high profile Nazis in their ranks over the years and all have been driven out by the Docks boys. They are **Nicky P** who was credited with coming up with the name Soul Crew, **Bollock** who fucked off to Northern Ireland

and **Mark Taylor** who only escaped by gassing some Docks boys when they tried to batter him in the Owain pub.

Swansea BNP

Swansea's Jacks have always been known as a far right firm, following the National Front in the 80's and 90's and the BNP now. They have never been too shy to Seig Heil in front of the cameras. This is discussed in the Swansea chapter. It must be stressed that everything discussed in this chapter relates to incidents in the Cardiff and Valleys area. The far right of Cardiff and Swansea could not get together even united by their love of politics and racism as the hatred between them is too great.

Nowadays

Beshella still lives in Maesteg although it's all gone quiet now. After he spent a few months inside for harassing a shopkeeper and was involved in a pub brawl in which an elderly lady died of a heart attack (he was cleared of any blame), it looks like he's trying to keep a low profile now.

Chapter Eleven
The Wales Scene

Well, where do I start? There's these four mobs, all supporting the national side, so the potential for trouble with opposing fans as well as each other is massive. The rivalry is so bad that when Wales played Slovenia at Swansea's Liberty stadium in 2005, Cardiff fans who are the largest part of the Wales following, had to be segregated from the other Welsh fans. Police had to triple their numbers to stop outbreaks of trouble even though Slovenia had hardly any fans there. One fan told journalists, "It kicked off between Swansea and Cardiff fans and was very nasty. It's a sad state of affairs when you have to segregate a country's fans."

Wales at Lucifer's Lounge

In 1973 the Home International Championships were an established part of the football calendar. At the end of every season the four home nations would battle it out for the prize of, well Home International Champions I suppose. Thanks to my Uncle Eifion, Tom and I were taken to our first Wales match at Wrexham's Racecourse Ground. The visitors were Scotland. I don't really remember much about the match itself. The visitors won 2-0 with a certain George Graham netting both goals. We were at the Kop end of the ground, trying our best to see over the bloody wall at the bottom. I remember being amazed at the amount of Scots at the match with all their yellow banners. I thought Scotland was just the other side of Tibet so Wrexham would have been a fair hike for them. Finally, when the Scotland team bus drove past, Big Jim Holton flicked the 'v's' at us. We were fucking twelve years old for god's sake!

The next time I was to see Wales play the Scots, it was to be in very different circumstances. A Home match but this time at Anfield. Home match, my arse. If ever the Welsh FA and Welsh public fucked up, then it was on this particular game. So how did all come about? Well, Wales in the previous European Championships campaign had reached the Quarter Finals. This stage of the tournament was then played on a home and away basis. They were drawn against the skilful but unpredictable Yugoslavians. Wales lost the away leg 0-2 so it was always going to be an uphill struggle in the home match. A large passionate crowd turned up at Ninian Park, determined to roar the Welsh through and into the semis. It all went sour after only 18 minutes though when the Yugoslavs were awarded a penalty. All hell broke loose. It degenerated into a farce. At one stage an irate fan chased the referee with one of the corner flags, hurling it at him like a spear. It was like a scene from Zulu. There was no 'Men of Harlech' to rescue us from this one and even though Wales did manage an equaliser amidst a horrible atmosphere, there was to be serious repercussions from UEFA for the crowd disorder. Wales were ordered to play their next home qualifying match at least 150 miles from Cardiff.

They'd already played Czechoslovakia at Wrexham and had a cracking 3-0 win, against the then European Champions. Their next home match was against Scotland, so the logical choice was again Wrexham. The tight Racecourse Ground had always been a tough place for any visiting side to come to. However, certain factors were conspiring against the Welsh side. Both sides still had a chance of qualifying for the World Cup to be held in Argentina and there was huge interest in the media and amongst the general public as both sides were from Britain. The Scots had massive support at the time. Only months earlier they'd took home the Wembley pitch and goal posts after a memorable win against their 'Auld Enemy'. I can only assume that the Welsh FA didn't fancy thousands of the Tartan Army descending on Wrexham and doing the same thing. Far be it for me to be cynical but Anfield held 50,000 at the time. Nearly double the Racecourse. The game was to go on in Liverpool.

Still, it was a home game for Wales so we should still have the Lions share of support. We had players like John Toshack who were more than used to playing at Lucifer's Lounge. What a joke. By hook or by crook the Jocks got hold of tickets by the shipload. Of the 50,000 crowd that evening, to me it seemed like they had 45,000. I wasn't far off. I was going up with a lad called Skell. He was a bit of a lad. He joined the Merchant Navy not long after but after going round the world a few times, catching the clap in various ports, he became bored and joined the Paras! Years later, on exercise in Canada he went AWOL. Finding his way to California, he ended up kipping rough on Venice Beach for three months. I could think of worse places to do it. He did come back to Britain eventually but was nicked after chucking a brick through the windows of the Bridgend Conservative Club. He was handed over to the army and had to do his time in Colchester Military Prison. Last I heard he was back in the States.

The day started off badly for yours truly. I wandered lonely round the streets of Port killing time before our lift to Liverpool. There I was, quietly contemplating life, when a coach load of lads stopped on the opposite side of the street to have a piss in the Public Loos. It was a bus full of lads from Pwllheli on their way to the match. Now, at the time there was a slight little war going on between Port and Pwllheli. You know, two little hick towns with nothing else to do but have a scrap. Too late, they spotted me. I was persona non grata at the time with their little mob and they had me in their sights. A quick decision was made and I thought it may be wise to do a runner. Linford Christie eat your heart out. I also had the advantage of knowing the lie of the land so I lost them pretty quickly round the back streets. I peered over a wall at one stage and saw them calling to each other, "Where is the bastard!" Not this time boys! Strangely, one of their main faces at the time was a lad called Kippax – a big Man City fan. He was eventually to marry a girl from Port and move there. Over the years, we were to become firm friends and still travel to watch Wales together. Not on this particular day though.

We were filled with trepidation and excitement on the way to Liverpool. Excitement at the thought that a Welsh win would put us within touching distance of qualifying but trepidation at the news that thousands of Welsh tickets had ended up in Scottish hands. Question to the people of Wales - how? The full horror was realised when we emerged from the Mersey Tunnel onto Scotland Road. The road from the tunnel to the ground was lined with thousands upon thousands of Scottish fans and they were all well pissed. This was a recipe for disaster.

After our driver eventually parked up, myself and Skell went on a little recce around. It was chaos. There were Jocks everywhere and if you didn't have at least an inch of Tartan on your body you were marked out. It was going to be a long night! The first Welsh we saw were in a coach from South Wales trying to wend its way towards the ground. The Jocks were trying to turn it into an exhibit for a vintage vehicle display while some of the lads at the back of the bus were piling out of the emergency exits to get amongst their attackers. We were just walking past at the time and this lad off the coach shouted, "Fuck off you Jock Cunt." I replied, "We're North Wales, mate." "Fuck off you North Walian Cunt then," was his retort. There were now three sets of fans going to this game, Scotland, North Wales and South Wales.

There were sporadic outbreaks of fighting all the way up to the Kop where our tickets were for. To add to it all, it was pitch black. Outside the ground, the queues were all over the place. There were people jumping queues, people falling pissed, people fighting, people abusing. You name it, it was going on that night. The Mounted Police were trying desperately to keep some semblance of order. This involved smacking anything that moved over the head with a truncheon. As crowd control went, this was as thankless a task as I could ever imagine. One copper grabbed my hair as I ducked under his horse to keep up with Skell. He pulled me up and 'Bang', contact with his Horse's head - OUCH!

When we eventually made it onto the terrace, our worst fears were proved correct. The whole ground seemed to be packed with Scots fans, certainly in our part of the Kop it was. Whatever support there was for Wales, eventually congregated in the top right hand corner. You could tell the South Walians. There were loads of them wearing miner's helmets, complete with lamps. Scrawled on the side, CCFC.

The passionate audience made sure that the match cracked and fizzled throughout. It really was one hell of a night. One that will live long in the memory. Pity it was for all the wrong reasons. While both sides battled on gamely, drunken brawls erupted on the Kop throughout. When empty whisky bottles started flying through the air, you knew it wasn't to stick your pennies in for Christmas. Broom sticks were taken off their flags and used as weapons. As a large gap appeared in the middle of the Kop, Skell and I saw our chance and were down on our knees picking up all the loose coins that everyone had been trying to chuck into the empty whisky bottles. We also collected a nice hoard of programmes which would give us a tidy little profit. The fighting raging all around us was way out of our league - these cunts had beards and 'nay teeth Jimmy'!

Toshack hit the bar for Wales but neither side could break the deadlock until the 78th minute. The ball sailed into the Welsh box down at the Anfield Road end of the ground. A clutch of players went up for it. Joe Jordan, the toothless gimp, stuck his hand out in a 'Harlem Globetrotteresque' manner. He caught the ball, juggled it a few times, did some keepy ups on the back of his neck, while the crowd looked on in disbelief. A Clive Thomas look-alike, otherwise known as Robert Wurtz from France, whistled.............. and pointed to the spot. Penalty, the twat had given them a penalty. Allegations abounded after the match that Mr Wurtz regularly holidayed on the banks of Loch Lomond in a property rented out by a Mr J Jordan. Why else would he have awarded such a ludicrous decision? Don Masson slotted home the spot kick. We called the ref all the names under the sun and the strains of 'Que Sera Sera' filled the night. The son of Satan, one Kenneth Mathieson Dalglish, made it 2-0 with a couple of minutes to go. It was immaterial. Welsh hearts had been broken by Jordan's blatant handball. Go into any bar in Wales to this day and Ann Robinson is a famous child of Wales compared to that bastard.

The only consolation, if it can be called that, was that the Scots made an early departure from the Argentine after being embarrassed by those footballing giants of Iran and Peru. Even then, they still managed to restore some pride by beating the Dutch 3-2 with one of the best goals you'll ever see. That dribble and shimmy from Archie Gemmill. The gods may well be conspiring though. Only recently, Scotland lost an important qualifier in Lithuania to a controversial penalty. I can't deny it. I had a wry grin as all the phone-ins went mad with bleating Jocks whinging about the referee. Where's Robert Wurtz when you need him eh?

Wales-Poland in Cardiff

Before this game there were arrests in Port Talbot, Neath, Bridgend and Cardiff as Jacks bumped into Cardiff groups all along the route. 30 Jacks entered the Red Lion pub outside Central Station which at the time was a well known gay haunt and started accusing drinkers of being Cardiff fans and attacking them. Typical.

Every time there is a Wales match, there is always trouble between the various Welsh mobs. In Milan, apart from the massive trouble in the ground after Italian police refused to stop the locals throwing piss, shit and bottles at the Welsh fans all the way through the game, there were several incidents of violence between Welsh firms as well. 15 Newport who had teamed up with Swansea Jacks were battered by a much larger group of Cardiff and one Newport fan was slashed down his side. In the Swansea book, Tooze talks about this incident only his version is that the Newport boys were done, then him and a small group of Jacks gave the Cardiff what for. Yeh ok mate!

Fact is, Swansea don't usually travel with Wales as they know they will get hassle off Cardiff lads and they can't deal with it. Newport and Wrexham usually do and there have been some legendary offs with these firms and Cardiff over the years but they've been well documented in other books so I won't repeat them here.

Wales v Slovakia by C Squad

After the game, most Cardiff headed back to Canton for a drink before hitting town. At about 8:00pm, a bunch of scruffy looking cunts in Burberry, Stone Island and Lonsdale gathered near the door of the boozer. Cardiff steamed out of the pub and the Slovaks had second thoughts and backed off. They ran to the other side of the road and tried standing again but got legged. After running them as far as Riley's snooker club everyone went back to the pub. Didn't expect them to pull a stunt like that but fair play for looking for it. They got more than they bargained for.

At a recent game in Cardiff, **Wales v Germany,** every time Cardiff had 15 boys drinking together, they were videoed and the amount of police on the streets was ridiculous. The Germans brought a firm although they were mostly scruffy bastards led by a Tooze style steroid hunk with 'Made in Germany' on his T-shirt. When some of the Cardiff asked them to meet up in Sophia gardens, they really didn't want to know. If you were over there and they had the numbers advantage though, they would have wanted it for sure.

As I've said, any game played in Cardiff at the moment is policed beyond all belief. There will always be trouble at Wales games abroad though, either between Taffies travelling to them and back or with the foreign devils who always seem to turn out for us. There have been some memorable battles involving Wales over the years and one of these was **Germany 1989 in Cologne.**

Meic tells the story:
"Deutschland Hooligans," they screamed as they neared us. We stood in front of them, an alliance of Bangor Warfare, Wrexham and Cardiff lads. They steamed into us, outnumbering us 3 to 1 with boots and fists flying. There were so many of them attacking us, they were hitting other Krauts in the confusion. We held off the Germans as wave after wave of attacks happened all day. It was mental but we had to stick together that day or we were fucked.

Another good one was the Holland game in **Amsterdam 1988.** Inside the stadium was about 800 of us including a firm of 300 made up of Soul Crew, Wrexham Frontline, Bangor Warfare, Newport and smaller North Walian firms. During the game there was the usual anti-Swansea chanting but the majority of the violence was from the Dutch end as **Ajax and Feyenoord** went toe-to-toe. At the final whistle, we steamed out of the stadium towards the Dutch mob. The ones that stood were slapped but most of their lads scattered into the darkness. On the whole the Dutch were very disappointing, considering they had clubs like Ajax, Feyenoord and Den Haag, all of whom had a hooligan following. We were basically able to go where we wanted and take the piss. Tooze says in his book that many Jacks don't bother to travel to Wales games seeing it as more of a Cardiff thing. What a load of crap. The truth is that every time they have turned up, it has kicked off between them and Cardiff so they don't bother as they don't want a shoeing. As you can see, the other Welsh mobs may team up in times of need but Cardiff and Swansea? It just wouldn't happen.

Milan
In Milan, as well as all the trouble in the ground, where the Old Bill received a

Cardiff at Burnley 80's.

Sam Hammam and some Soul Crew lads.

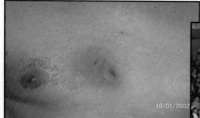

A Cardiff lad's chest after Ajax stabbed him with a sharpened Brolly.

Wolves in the Grange end (above).

Birmingham Zulus in the Grange end (left).

Report on the trouble at pre-season friendly v Merthyr 2008 (above).

GATLAND BLASTS HIS SIDE AFTER BOKS CRUSH WALES

Hooligans promise bloodshed at Welsh derby

VILE VIDEO'S
EXCLUSIVE
By ANDREW BAGNELL

CALL TO ARMS

Cardiff and Swansea slam disgraceful 'Nazi' film

EXPRESS **SPORT**

IT'S NOT SO VERY FRIENDLY

by DAVID WILLIAMS

But future of Cardiff City fixture looks secure despite eruption of violence

Wales on Sunday report about Youtube video allegedly stirring up trouble at a forthcoming Cardiff v Swansea derby.

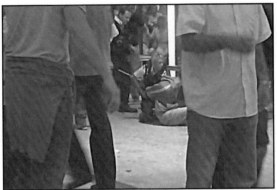

Arrests after the clash between Cardiff and FC Twente (above).

CARDIFF CITY SOUL CREW
BRIDGEND TOWN FIRM

KEEP THE FAITH

Dave Jones
co-author of 'Soul Crew'
in 80's.

CARDIFF VS POMPEY

THE SHEEP SHAGGERS ARE COMING

17TH OF MAY 2008

STARRING GRAY WOLF & BROWN BEAR WITH WHITE RABBIT PRODUCED BY WHITE RABBIT & GRAY WOLF DIRECTOR OF PHOTOGRAPHY GRAY WOLF & BROWN BEAR FILM EDITED BY BROWN BEAR & GRAY WOLF MUSIC BY WHITE RABBIT PRODUCTION DESIGN BY GRAY WOLF COSTUME DESIGN BY BROWN BEAR WRITTEN & DIRECTED BY WHITE RABBIT

Powered by Poster Forge

The author with Martin King and Annis
at launch of
'From Shattered Dreams to Wembley Way'.

Cardiff v Swindon.

Valleys Lads in Blackpool.

*Cardiff lads (right) and in
Southampton (above).*

Bangor CCFC Lads (below).

Scarfer hurt when Sheffield Utd bricked the coaches.

Old Bill in Harrow after the wrecking and thieving spree by scarfers.

Trouble at Wales v Germany 1990 in Cardiff.

FC Twente in Cardiff.

Cardiff searching the backstreets for Millwall 2000.

The Invisible Empire.

Racist literature that was sold
around the Valleys in the 90's.

The Grand Wizard
Allan Beshella.

Charlie Sargent, racial instigator and police informer in the 90's.

Through to the final,
what a turnup.

It's all gone mental as Pompey
steam in.

Cardiff's Firm in Kilburn.

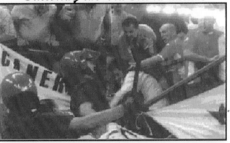

Battering the Old Bill in Milan.

Famous Cardiff face 'Dick the
Docker' in the Marine days.

Something you wouldn't expect in the
21ˢᵗ century....
getting covered in spit and piss
at a football match in the San Siro!

Nope, the Soul Crew hadn't been here before us.... only NATO! We inspect the damage post-war in Belgrade.

Me waiting for Swansea.

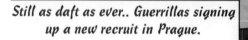

Still as daft as ever.. Guerrillas signing up a new recruit in Prague.

Cardiff Lads.

serious hiding after refusing to stop the Italian fans raining down bottles, etc on the Welsh fans, there was serious bother between the various factions of Taffies. Fifteen Newport teamed up with Tooze and his mates and were battered by a larger group of Cardiff which ended with one of them being stabbed. Seems the Welsh fans just can't get on wherever they play. Word is that the Newport were singled out for a really serious hiding after having jumped Annis when he was on his own with a girl at a pre-season friendly in Newport - See photo in Newport chapter.

Cardiff's Firm at Wales Games by Annis Abraham
Author of 'From Shattered Dreams to Wembley Way' and 'Diary of the Real Soul Crew'
Over the last 35 years, I've mainly followed Cardiff City as that is my club and always will be. But I've also seen Wales, England and Scotland abroad. Over the years I've probably been to over 100 Wales games and during those years, Cardiff has always had the main firm present. I'm not saying that just because I'm Cardiff but I don't bullshit. It's just the plain truth. For a while Cardiff and Wrexham had their battles with each other during the 80's and fair play to Wrexham, they were always outnumbered but they always had a good go. That's behind us now and usually we drink in the same pubs at Wales games. If it was a Cardiff v Wrexham game, well that's a completely different matter.

The Jacks and Newport. Well that's a totally different ballgame as most Cardiff will never accept either firm. There are a couple of lads like Pricket (Newport County) who is old school and it goes back to the 80's where there's mutual respect but that's as far as it goes. As for Swansea, not one has ever been allowed to drink in the same pub as Cardiff abroad. The truth of the matter is, I've only ever seen Jacks at about eight out of the 100 Wales games I've attended and six of the games were down in Jackland.

One of the games I will never forget was **Wales v Spain at Wrexham 1985**, a night game. I'd gone on the train to this game with my mates, Mannings, Beer, Richard E etc. About 100 Cardiff were on this train, a lot of older heads too. When we arrived at Wrexham at about lunchtime, we found a pub straightaway and settled in. The pub soon became a free for all as the dozy landlord had left his stockroom open and some of the lads were just passing crates of beer out to others. Within a few hours the lads were soon pissed up and as the day went on, our numbers grew to around 750, all of them Cardiff lads. With about half an hour to kick-off, myself and around half a dozen others left the pub and made our way to the ground. We made it there with no problems and were soon standing on the Kop end which is Wrexham's home terrace.

The ground was buzzing as it was a 30,000 sell-out. One minute you would hear, "Wales, Wales" next minute, "Wrexham, Wrexham." The seven of us went, "Kairdiff, Kairdiff" and within seconds a bit of a toe-to-toe was happening between us and the locals. We were well outnumbered and took quite a few punches but it didn't stop us standing our ground. We gave as good as we received. All of a sudden, we heard a massive roar of "Kaiirdiff" behind us and over 200 Cardiff came pouring into the Kop. They had come through the turnstiles, waited till they were all in then all come in together. Now it was game on. The locals soon backed off, some just disappearing into the packed crowd, the rest just went silent. Now all you could hear was Cardiff songs and soon more and more had come, swelling our numbers to well over 400 lads. The Old Bill put a line between us and the rest of the Welsh crowd. We were all congregated to the side of the Kop near the entrance.

The game kicked off and our numbers were still increasing with lads from Bangor, Holyhead and other parts of North Wales joining us. As far as we are concerned, these areas have always been Cardiff followers and still do to this present day. On some big games over the years, they have even brought full coaches of lads to our games and they have some very game lads. Everything had now calmed down when suddenly about 60 lads entered the Kop. All I heard was, "They're fucking Jacks," and with that all hell broke loose. They never had a chance. They were smashed before they could even try to have a go back. The Old Bill now had a big problem. They had to separate the end into three sections. It was a sight to see, three long lines of Police and three different mobs.

Cardiff went quiet for a while and the Old Bill started to relax their guard. Suddenly, Wales scored and as the ground erupted into celebration. Cardiff just steamed straight through the line of Old Bill, smashing the Jacks once more. This happened every time we scored and the game ended 3-nil to Wales so the Jacks took another few hidings.

At the end of the game, the Old Bill seemed lost about what to do with us. I remember a lad called Ducky of the band 'Oppressed' get together his mob who were mostly from Grangetown and managed to get right behind the Jacks and followed them back to their coach. The rest of us had been forced back by police with batons and dogs. I later heard the Grangetown lads had steamed the Jacks by the coaches and had got right into them and given them a proper pasting. We were all eventually escorted back to the train station by the ground. Well, there you go. The Jacks tried their best to support Wales but back then Cardiff never let them and it seems they never will.

Wales v England by C Squad

The highly anticipated game between Wales and England was met with the highest police presence that the Welsh capital has ever seen for a sporting event. Police from all over the country were drafted to Cardiff to prevent any potential trouble. The game was given a 'Category C' rating. This is the highest rating a football match can be given by the police. England as expected sold their ticket allocation of 7,000 with many predicting plenty more Englishmen to turn up without a ticket. At around 10:00am, Welsh fans started to congregate in the gatekeeper pub opposite the stadium. Even at this time in the morning, Wales easily had 250 lads out without exaggeration. With the booze at full flow, more Welshmen started to enter the pub. Mainly Cardiff with a few Wrexham, no Swansea or Newport may I add.

The local Police force made their way into the pub mainly to suss out the numbers. Then around 12:30pm, a shout went out and about 50 made their way out of the pub. A few English had slipped through the police and made it to the pub. They ran into the middle of the road, threw a few bricks and bottles and run off as the mob made their way to them. They quickly ran down the road to the direction of the castle. 3:00am come and it was time for the game. The Welsh booed, jeered and whistled the English anthem to the point where you couldn't hear yourself speak. A closely fought game was played out in front of the 72,000 fans with England just scraping a win. As the English celebrated, something was going on in the stands. Some English had tickets for the Welsh stand. As they celebrated, they were kicked and punched down rows of seats. Not the day they bargained for in the land of the Sheep Shaggers.

After the game, main faces, old and new, made their way to the City Arms, mobbed up and made their way to the Goat Major in St. Mary's Street. The police started to take liberties bossing innocent Welsh fans around. That tipped it off. The Welsh lads steamed straight into the Old Bill eventually backing them off. Then more police came round the corner and backed off the Welshmen. In the night, no English hung around which made for a quiet night for the hundreds of Taffies. A handful of arrests were made mainly for drunk and disorderly behaviour. Swansea made some claims that they smashed up the borough but windows were still intact. All in all a good day.

Chapter Twelve
The Road to Wembley

Cardiff v Barnsley at Wembley FA Cup Semi's 2008

Ok, we made it through to the semi's. Might as well make the most of it as it's very unlikely we'll get to the final. Our luck on the pitch is poxed. We piled onto the Docker's coach from Barry, 8:00am, Seaside Section flag in tow and off we went. The ale was flowing before we'd even left Barry. This was tops. The Sheep Shaggers are on their way to Wembley. Now, although we aren't going for trouble, we know in the back of our minds that when Barnsley came to Cardiff, they had a good mob of over 100 lads who were up for it and as everyone hates us, the potential for trouble was there.

After many cans, we arrived in Harrow intending to have a good drink there, then walk on masse to Wembley. After about half an hour in the boozer, a small group of us decided we were bored and we set off on the walk to the ground alone. When we arrived at Harrow, Cardiff's scarfers had wrecked the place. Pubs had been trashed and shops looted. A chicken had been stolen from Iceland and was being booted back and forwards across the road. Just after our arrival, the heavy mob of Old Bill arrived so we decided to move away. Getting nicked for this disorderly behaviour was a waste of time.

As we passed a pub, a Valleys lad says, "This pub here's full of Barnsley," so we decided to go in for a pint. There was six of us and a pub full of Barnsley and although most of them were scarfers or barmies, there was a good 20-30 lads in there. We stood over in the corner and they were all chanting, "sheep sheep sheep shaggers" at us and we are just standing there, laughing at them. Eventually I noticed that more and more of them are turning up. They are on their mobiles, calling for help. There was only six of us for fuck's sake! We decided if it went off here, we were going to be cut to ribbons with the glasses that would be flying. We decided to take our pints and cockily walked out through the front doors. As we did, around ten of them came running out behind us. This one big bloke came towards us and I threw my full pint straight into his face. This shocked him to fuck and as he wiped the foam out of his eyes and stepped forward to have a go, he realised I had the glass held up, as if to say, "Take another step and this will be in your face, boyo." Some black Barnsley lad came bouncing out doing a boxing stance and the others looked at him and grinned at us as if to say, "You're in trouble now." When our boys charged forward, he shit himself and backed off and they all bottled it. What a bunch of bullying cunts. They thought we were going to run and because we didn't, they didn't know what to do. That's typical of today's 'hooligans'. Most are just bully arseholes who like terrorizing people while the numbers are in their favour. No bottle at all!

D's story

"Barnsley had 120 dressed lads drinking in Covent Garden. This is probably the same mob that were filmed in Cardiff last time. They were surrounded by Old Bill. 30 of them managed to get away and boarded a train. Unknown to them, a group of around 30 of Cardiff's top boys were on the same train but in a different carriage. Two Cardiff lads went for a wander through the carriages and on entering the Barnsley carriage, were set upon and took a right kicking. When the train pulled in at Leicester Square, the injured Cardiff stepped off. When the other Cardiff lads saw the state of them, they jumped off led by Richard E, ran down to where the Barnsley wankers were. "There's been a big misunderstanding," one of the shithouses said. "There's no misunderstanding here you cunts, you've been bullying and now it's payback time." The Cardiff lads kicked and beat absolute fuck out of them as they screamed for mercy. Have that you cunts!"

The only other trouble this day were little incidents scattered around but nothing major. Two of our lot were attacked by ten Barnsley outside Wembley Tube and a 14 year old kid was hit full in the back by a brick thrown by a Barnsley fan in his 30's. I bet he's proud of himself. All in all, Barnsley are crap. A shit excuse for a firm who couldn't even dish out a kicking to six of us when they had a pub full. Anyway, fuck me, we beat them and we're through to the final. First time in 81 years. We couldn't believe it! We'll have to come back to Wembley again now. It's a hard life innit!

Cardiff v Pompey FA Cup Final 2008

Of all the teams we could have ended up playing, we had to have Portsmouth, our old hated rivals from the 80's. For weeks before, the internet was alive with 'keyboard warriors' threatening mayhem. 'Cardiff will die', etc. Badges were produced with 'Casuals Cup Final, Soul Crew v 657 Crew' and the police were on the telly and radio bleating about how there will be 'zero tolerance' policing on the day. Well, as we all know, Cardiff don't like zero tolerance policing. We have this chip on our shoulders (more like a bag of spuds) about English Old Bill harassing us for being Welsh. Nicking Cardiff fans for minor offences like drinking, etc is a recipe for a riot as well they should know.

We hired a minibus and off we went. 8:00am start again and on the ale. One of our lot, Digger, had been up all night and was absolutely wrecked. He had been thrown out of a café that morning and was absolutely bonkers. There were 16 of us in this van and unlucky for us, they gave us a Muslim driver. Just our fucking luck! This boring twat moaned about our music, was telling people off about drinking, etc and then refused to take us to Kilburn which was where all the lads were due to meet. I had to have a serious word with the cunt and remind him we'd paid a lot of money for this minibus (twice the normal rate as it was for Wembley) and if he didn't take us where we wanted to go, he'd be leaving the minibus. He phoned his head office and it was (supposedly) sorted. Trouble was, when he made it to London and hit the traffic system, he was fucked! He said he'd never driven out of Barry before and was lost. For fuck's sake! We saw a tube station sign and jumped out, telling him to pick us up outside Gate 5 Bar after the game.

We travelled up to **Kilburn** and while we were walking down the road, some fucking Valley Commandoes bumped us as they passed. I turned round and they had recognized some of our group and were talking to them. I walked up and stood there and the ones who had bumped us didn't even say, "Sorry boys, I didn't know you were Cardiff." I was fucking fuming. If it hadn't been for the police in large numbers around, this bully wanker would have woken up with a crowd round him. It seems to be happening all the time with Cardiff lately, bully twats going round picking on small groups or people on their own.

Anyway, Cardiff's mob here was massive (see photos). At least 500 lads and all the top faces from the old days. Had Pompey tried to attack this pub, they would have died in the gutter. We didn't know it at the time but Pompey had sent spotters up to Kilburn and when they saw how many Cardiff there were, they reported back. Pompey by all accounts don't have that many boys interested in fighting these days and any idea they had to try and have a go at Cardiff was scrapped as a bad idea!

We all marched down to the tube station and made our way to the ground, a massive mob of lads and loads of scarfers and embarrassing cunts in funny hats, etc. The only problem we had on arrival was that me and Avo never had tickets! We walked about for a while trying to find a tout but demand for tickets was so high for this, we had no chance. Now the last time we had been to Wembley, we had had a few pints in Gate 5 Bar which at the Barnsley game had been allocated for Cardiff fans, so we headed there. We walked in and spoke to this big black bouncer who was an Arsenal lad. We had been chatting to him last time and he was massive. He said, "Sorry lads, it's all Pompey in here today." We said, "Come on mate, we've got nowhere else to go." He said we could go in as long as we kept a low profile. Inside they had a massive screen showing the game and there were about 90 Pompey in there, mostly scarfers but about 20 or so Lads. They were all singing, "Play up Pompey" and we are stood by the bar, trying not to look conspicuous. It was written all over us that we were Taffies. I remembered there was a beer garden and we decided to go out there. As I walked out through the door, I could see about 15 Casuals and there were probably more. A sharp turnaround was made and back in we went. We stood at the bar near the bouncers. We figured that if it did kick off, at least the bouncers would wade in to help us giving us more of a chance.

By now, nearly everyone in the pub was aware of us and we were getting some evil looks. We could have left but why should we? My Grandad didn't fight the Krauts so I can't go into a pub for a drink. Anyway, we're Cardiff, we have our pride. After Pompey scored, it really started looking like we were going to be filled in any second so we left through the front doors. We'd arranged to meet our minibus outside here and Avo starts ringing the boys to tell them where we are. Two Pompey came out and started mouthing. I said, "Us two and you two then. Let's go round the lane big boy." They said, "You want it, do you?" and ran back inside. Now it's on top! There's loads of them and only us two. Five minutes went past and no sign of them and a few of the lads from our bus turned up. There's 8 of us now, just stood round waiting for our bus. I'd forgotten all about Pompey in my drunken state. All of a sudden, the doors crash open and thirty of them come pouring out of the pub. I don't know if they expected us to run or what but we just stood there looking at them and they all froze and didn't seem to know what to do. I said, "Oh I get it, all you lot are gonna beat us up are you? That's brave of you."

Obviously thirty wasn't enough for them so some of them are on their mobiles calling for back up. More and more Pompey come flying down the steps from the ground and before long there has to be fifty plus lads and loads more scarfers all stood around mouthing off. No-one seems to have the bottle to start. I said, "Call this a 657 Crew? You're a fucking joke mob, all you lot and you wanna do us, you just ain't got the bottle." As I said this, one of them comes towards me swinging punches saying, "Come on then" and as I stepped forward to defend myself. 'Bang'. I'm punched from behind and on my arse I go. I stood straight back up and I'm windmilling into them and I feel this stinging pain in my knee but didn't know what it was at the time. As soon as the guy had hit me, two of my mates had laid into him and now there's a mass brawl going on. See the photos if you think I'm full of shit. Eight of us are fighting for our lives now against over 50 of Pompey's top boys. A young Casual in his twenties broke away from a scuffle and came towards me and I smacked him flying. As I did, 'bang' I'm hit from behind again and down again. This time I'm being booted by about five of them. There's no way I'm gonna stay down so they can use me for a Taffy bouncy castle though and I'm straight back up on my feet. By now the Old Bill are there and it's mayhem. My mate the black bouncer has chinned one of the ones who hit me on the sly and the police are beating back the Pompey hordes. An older Pompey guy, probably in his 50's in a Barber coat was shouting to his mates, "You're out of order Pompey, there's only a few of them."

I'm fucked now with concussion, hand ripped open, cut lip and bruises all over me. We made off and walked back to the station. One of our lot phoned the van driver and told him he'd have to pick us up at Kilburn and we set off across the tubes back to the pub we'd been in earlier. We had a scuffle with some more bullies from Pompey on the tube because we intervened when they picked on some scarfers and I was nearly arrested until the copper saw I was covered in blood and black and blue and let us go. On the journey home, I was fucked from all the head blows I'd taken. I later found out the stinging pain in my knee was the result of a copper lashing me with a telescopic cosh from behind which had me limping for the next six weeks. I ended up spewing in a bag on the way home. I was in a hell of a state.

K's story
"On the way back after losing to Pompey, a van full of Cardiff lads pulled into the services and as soon as they parked, were confronted by a van full of Pompey, all pissed up and mouthy as fuck. They had no idea who was in our van as they bounced across the car park with all the 'come on sheep shaggers' caper. The doors opened and within seconds they were being seriously battered. Several of them were pouring blood as they scrambled back into their van as punches and kicks rained down on them. They weren't getting away that fucking easy and we piled into the van and chased the cunts down the motorway. We stalked them for ages, bumper to bumper and we could see the fear on their faces as they thought they'd never escape. After about 50 miles we let them go, fucking idiots. That was a lesson they won't fucking forget in a hurry."

My verdict on Pompey is, fuck me, what a comedown from the mob they had in the 80's. They mouth off on the internet then when it comes down to it, they bully a small group and couldn't even give us a proper hiding. I'm not exaggerating but if we had the other eight from our van, we would have ended up chasing them.

The Trouble With Taffies

That's how bottleless they were in my opinion. From the photos, I've been shown the twat who smacked me from behind. All I can say is this, if I ever see him at a book launch or any Casuals do, he's gonna find out what it feels like to be smacked from behind, the spineless cunt. End of discussion.

Cardiff lost the game too (we were robbed) so our Wembley dream was over but we had some fun trips to remember and there's always next time. Bring it on.

Chapter Thirteen
Urban Guerrillas

For most football fans, the Severn Valley running through the heart of Mid Wales represents a rural no-man's land for weary northern football firms heading south for a nervy afternoon at either Ninian Park or The Liberty. To the uninitiated, the terrain is classic sheep shagging country and the locals are cruelly branded as nothing more than walk-on extras for a remake of Deliverance. But think again because there is a formidable football crew in them there hills. Dotted either side of the A483 are villages which are home to some of Wales's most loyal soldiers who, when the call is made, have no problem in mustering 200 troops with passport and beer money in hand, ready to drink any European city dry. Defending Wales is in the locals' blood and ancestry. Some of Wales's fiercest battles with the invading English were fought in and around these villages some 600 years ago and little has changed since. You will see more 'Royal Welsh' standards flying here than Welsh Dragons and as you venture further inland, God help you if you wonder into the wrong pub with a Brummie or a Scouse accent. These days, that overwhelming sense of loyalty is channelled towards the principality's football side and the lads of Abermule, Berriew, Llanfair, Caersws, Llanfyllin and Guilsfield have become local legends.

Growing up in Mid Wales makes you feel like a second class citizen to the big cities but ask most of them now if they would have wanted it any different and you'll be lucky to leave with a full set of teeth. Rural passion and pride runs through the veins of every one of us and although some have left for careers in the big cities, the magnetic draw of the villages sees us all return at some point through the year.

Our firm is no different. Growing up in the late 1980's was an interesting time. Guilsfield is just a short hop across the border from Shrewsbury which was brimming with birds and boozers; paradise compared to the limited selection of farmers' daughters and mates' sisters that were cramming into the village's pair of pubs. Soul Music was big and so was football hooliganism and in Shrewsbury one of the most impressive football firms had emerged from the tough housing estates - The English Border Front (EBF). Shrewsbury Town may have been a family club that played at the Gay Meadow but there was nothing batty about the EBF who were one of the most well organised mobs in the country. Some say they had tied up the town's drug market during the 'E' boom and few would be brave enough to argue any different.

But what made this firm formidable was their ability to sniff out Welsh blood the second it strayed over the border from Powys into Shropshire. We had to learn fast. We always knew to travel in unmarked mini buses or taxis, to keep our mouths shut and most of all to stay in groups but after a few lagers, the draw of the bright lights saw us split up and many a good night was capped off by an EBF assault on the Indian Restaurant we were gathered in or at the bus stop where we waited for our lift home.

It was dangerous stuff at times and nights out to Shrewsbury were being meticulously planned with military precision to ensure everyone returned home in one piece. But we did wise up. Some of the older lads in the village had been following Wales for a few years and one day in 1989, we were gathered in the Oak pub and listening to the stories told about their recent trip to Denmark. They had spent 20 hours on a rollercoaster ferry journey and within an hour of landing they were attacked by local skinheads. I remember looking around the table and seeing my mates' eyes wide open as we listened to every word. But even a story of a brutal beating had a funny side. The lads were heavily outnumbered and their legs were still like jelly from the ferry trip as the blows rained down from dozens of loopy locals. And yet, all he could remember was looking up from the floor and seeing one of his mates blending in with the skinheads and putting the boot in too!

"What did you expect mate? For me to take a beating too?" was his defence. We laughed for hours and all of us decided we wanted a piece of it. So the village firm was born. The Guilsfield and District Urban Guerrillas had joined the ranks of the Soul Crew, The Jacks and the Wrexham Frontline as Wales's latest football firm and these were definitely the boys I wanted alongside me as we began our European exploits. With recruits from the village itself and the surrounding farms and hamlets, we looked the part. Lads are made bloody big in the country. Arms shaped from working as soon as you can walk and the summer barn dance free-for-alls providing perfect grounding for looking after yourself on the streets of Brussels, Belgrade or Baku. Let me get something straight, the Guerrillas are not trouble-makers but trouble-sorters. Not one of the crew would ever look for trouble - never has and never will - but if it came his way, there would be a band of brothers standing firm to defend its ground in a way our forefathers did to repel the English all those centuries ago. As I said... it is in our blood and ancestry.

The crew came of age in 1990 when a few of us joined the 'founding fathers' on the train trip to Luxembourg for a European Championship qualifier. We wanted to sample what these lads had been telling us about on Saturday nights and all I can say is that 20 years later, the same bunch of daft sods still make the backbone of the crew's trips to Wales matches abroad!

There was one moment on that initial trip that has become legendary and is recounted time and time again in the departure lounges of airports three or four times a year. I guess you could say it underlined our naivety at the time as we were totally oblivious to the internal strife in Wales between the Swansea and Cardiff fans - The Jacks and the Soul Crew. We had indulged in three days of solid laugh-a-minute boozing and even saw Rushy secure a 1-0 win against one of the real heavyweights of European football (note the sarcasm) and we were sitting in the ferry port of Ostend killing time in the early hours. There were a dozen of us and some are big lads - gentle giants but nevertheless easy targets. We noticed there was a big group of lads and identified them as Cardiff fans by the shirt one was wearing. They looked tough - bloody tough. One of my mates decided to go and get a can of pop from out of the vending machine which was close to them and he walked past. The Cardiff lads mistakenly saw it as some sort of goading and one of them stood up and followed my mate to the machine. The lad had a Welsh Dragon tattooed on the side of his shaved head and we were alerted to the brewing trouble by one of our founding fathers who had sniffed trouble from the off.

As my mate was fumbling for coins to buy a can of Dr Pepper, the lad walked up behind him and said,

"Are you Jacks?" Somewhat shocked, my mate replied,
"Sorry mate?"
"You heard me, are you Jacks?"
Without even sensing the trouble that was possibly seconds away, my mate replied innocently, "No mate, it is Jacques… Mark Jacques."

You could not have scripted it better. The Dr Pepper dropped from the machine, he picked it up as cool as a cucumber and walked past the Cardiff lad who was completely perplexed saying 'cheers' as he went by and raised the can to the others who were equally stunned. When he returned to us, he simply said, "I think that lad knows me from somewhere." It was priceless. Thankfully there was no trouble.

We were hooked and since that day, more Wales matches than not have included a crew from the Guilsfield and District Urban Guerrillas. The net has widened. Some of us have moved abroad and others have chased their careers across the country which has made the Wales-away get togethers even more important. The lads are not bonded by following a specific football club, only the national team. Growing up in Mid Wales unfortunately leads you to supporting the team you see on television rather than Welsh clubs. After all, you can get to Wolverhampton, Everton, Liverpool and Manchester in half the time it takes to reach Cardiff or Swansea. A few follow Wrexham to be fair.

The crew has created a sense of togetherness that is hard to explain to anyone that has not experienced it. Never has a bad word been said between us except when someone stalls on a round and the antics we have got up to over the years are the stuff of local folklore.

That same campaign as Luxembourg, we undertook an even more arduous train journey to Germany to watch the fateful final qualifier. We were full of confidence for the long journey (as we always are) as Rushy's famous strike had seen us beat the reigning World Cup winners 1-0 in Cardiff. Thousands made the trip. Probably Wales's biggest mob abroad until Milan in 2004 and tickets were scarce. The match was to be played in Nuremberg which was skinhead central with Nazism still as popular then as Turkish kebab shops are today. We couldn't get tickets but one bloke in the village had hosted a local German football youth team from Frankfurt (about three hours away) that year in an international tournament and had sorted us out. The only problem was that we had to meet him in a hamburger bar in Frankfurt the night before the match.

So we planned our itinerary to head there and, remember, these were the days before internet and mobile phones and the only way of finding this bloke was through a group picture our local contact had given us. The guy's head was the size of a pin prick in the picture but nevertheless, we were confident. We arrived at the hamburger bar and time passed without our contact showing. One beer, then two, three were added to the dozen we had already consumed that afternoon before one of the older lads came up with the quote of the century. He was the one that had organised the tickets and had been conspicuously quiet for some time before piping up....

"Lads, I have a terrible thought. Maybe we were supposed to meet this bloke in a frankfurter bar in Hamburg and not a hamburger bar in Frankfurt?"

Luckily the guy showed. Our seats were slap bang in the middle of the German end and thanks to an inspired implosion by Gavin Maguire, Wales lost 4-0 but win or lose we are on the booze and we drank non-stop for 15 hours back to Ostend which was becoming our second home!

The lads have moved on in life. Some have married, divorced, married again and many have kids. The ranks include accountants, journalists, senior management, engineers and even a royal advisor but when the call is made, the Guilsfield and District Urban Guerrillas unite and the good times roll as if we were together the day before. Trips to Serbia, Italy, Finland and Ireland have seen huge increases in numbers with a new generation joining the brotherhood. Good lads that have adopted the message of trouble-sorters and not trouble-makers.

The whole Severn Valley though is a bedrock of Welsh football fanaticism. While scarcely has there been a game without representation from The Guerrillas, the same can be said for those other villages. Most of them we know from school or work and even played football with. Good, decent lads who ensure there is a strong sense of camaraderie running throughout Montgomeryshire.

It came to the fore back in 2004 when the news filtered through that one of the Llanfyllin lads, Martyn Digwood, had been seriously injured in a car incident in Turin. We were already in Milan for the match. Lads from all over the county were contacting each other to try and find out information. We were told he was hit by a car whilst crossing the road and that he was seriously injured. The unbelievable news of his death was confirmed to us the very next day. He was a superb lad. One of those lads that everyone had a good story to look back on. He was full of life, loved Wales, football and his family. He is still missed by one and all.

It seems that as we have grown older we have just become dafter! In one unnamed European city, what started as a collection of cones pilfered from a road works culminated in flashing traffic lights, road signs and even a 10-foot safety barrier filling one of our rooms. God knows what the maid must have thought after we checked out!

But the sinister side of football came to the fore once again in the Czech Republic. The lure of Prague had ensured the old crew was back to full strength. Toshack's revolution and the perennial optimism of a fresh campaign had persuaded thousands of Taffies to head east. While the world's football authorities seem to have thrown the book at British club and countries over the last 20 years for hooliganism, backwaters like Eastern Europe continue to have a free hand to do whatever they want. Even in this day and age, we witnessed the police doing monkey chants for our black players in Serbia. They soon shut up when we replied with chants of U-S-A! Those NATO bombings were still fresh in the memory and had struck a chord.

Prague was horrific. Well, not so much Prague but the shit hole called Teplice where the Czech FA had decided to host the game. It was an industrial town that had hit hard times three hours from the capital and something wasn't right from the moment we arrived. It was so grey it made the Rhondda shine like Vegas in comparison. The Guerrillas organised our own bus from Prague at around 2:00pm for an 8:00pm kick-off and the bulk of the other Welsh lads were due to leave in an organised convoy at 4:00pm. We thought we'd get there early, find a decent boozer and let the fun begin. We were unaware that the local authorities had advised the Welsh to arrive as late as possible due to a hard core hooligan element which thrived in this arse end of hell.

There were about 15 of us from The Guerrillas and a few lads from other local villages. The rest of the seats were filled up with couples and even a family or two looking to enjoy the late summer sun in a picturesque part of Europe. But while Prague was the epitome of a stunning city, Teplice was grim. It was the Quasimodo of towns and there was an eerie sense of emptiness as we drove past the deserted factories and smoke towers. We asked the driver to take us to the centre but it was the classic tumbleweed town as graffiti covered just about any spare inch of wall that could be found. What people you did see had wrinkled, weathered faces and only broke their sallow stare at the ground with a brief look at the first foreigners that had probably entered town since the Second World War!

Despite the cheap Czech lager that we had already consumed in copious amounts, you couldn't help but feel uneasy; even more so when you saw the worried faces of the women and children looking from out of the bus window at Shitville. As we continued to drive around, in the distance we saw a welcome and encouraging sight. There was a boozer surrounded by what looked like lads wearing red so we told the driver to halt and offloaded, setting a course for the pub.

What we didn't know was that the pub had half a dozen Welsh boys trapped inside and a cordon of riot police had surrounded it and the lads we saw in red were locals trying to fight their way in. It transpired that a spotter had clocked the Welsh lads going into the pub and before they knew it, 100 of the meanest looking lads had hit them from every entry and battered the crap out of them. Riot police managed to turf them out but it was still a cowardly attack on some decent North Wales lads. We were walking straight towards them. Before we realised what was going on, it was too late. The call went up to attack and the next thing we knew, this evil looking cross breed of Phil Mitchell and Ghandi's scrotum was steaming straight into us. The lads stood firm. Where the hell was there to leg it to anyway? The kids and women were absolutely terrified and took shelter behind the bus as the boys prepared for the first wave.

On getting nearer, the skinheads saw the size of some of our lads and their pace slowed. Maybe they were shocked that lads were willing to stand their ground but their sprint became a jog and then a walk with arms out goading our boys to attack them! Some of us, driven on by thirst for the pub, were some distance ahead and were surrounded by the locals and it became very unpleasant but by the time the riot police charged into them with truncheons flying, the Guerrillas had won some serious kudos and respect from this cesspit of Europe. When we stepped into the pub and saw the lads who had been on the end of the beating, it became apparent that we were in for an interesting afternoon. Just like the lads under Davy Crockett's command, we engineered a plan to defend our Alamo because we really did not have a place to go. Thankfully it was a glorious afternoon so we were drinking outdoors.

We could see their spotters all over and in the distance we could also make out small gangs assembling and we were expecting an attack from all angles at any minute. Some lads were given jobs to act as lookouts. At the first sign of an attack, the women and kids were told to just get inside the pub and we'd try and hold off until the fuzz arrived. There wasn't another Welsh fan in town at that time. Text messages were going back and forward to Prague for reinforcements but they were still two hours away. It was one of the most unsettling times we've had following football. The locals were like savages but thankfully the Old Bill was even worse and took no prisoners literally when they were sorting them out. It was brutal stuff.

By the time the rest of the lads arrived and took over the town's square, the locals were on the back foot and when news came through that the Cardiff lads had sorted out a few, it was music to our ears.

The Guilsfield and District Urban Guerrillas may not boast the biggest numbers and certainly hasn't earned a reputation as one of the country's most notorious crews. But what it does have is the sort of solidarity that is prevalent in every football firm the length and breadth of Britain. Long may it continue to keep the faith and should Wales finally qualify for a major tournament, expect the villages of Montgomeryshire to be deserted!

Cardiff City fan David Williams is the author of the best selling hooligan thriller 'Desert England' and 'Bring on the Soul Crew' (released 2009).

See www.desertengland.com

Chapter Fourteen
Other Mobs

Here's my opinion of various other mobs over the years.

Chelsea

In the 70's and 80', Chelsea caused Cardiff's mob more grief than anyone else. Turning up in massive numbers and taking on all comers. One of the Cardiff lads C tells the story of their raid on Cardiff early 80's. "It was kicking off all through the game, it was mental. Outside, the Chelsea hordes were taking it to Cardiff big time. The Cockneys were very organised, unlike us and they were smashing Cardiff and Valleys lads all down Sloper road. At the time I was 17 and was terrified. Every time Cardiff regrouped to go back into them, they were going through us like an army unit even though we had some fucking hard boys with us. We couldn't deal with their numbers and organisation. We regrouped in massive numbers under the tunnel by the Ninian Pub and they came back at us. I could see their front line were all blokes in their 30's and try as we might, they just beat us back. Some of the older guys were so frustrated I swear they had tears in their eyes. A few Cardiff were stabbed up as well which made the whole day much more frightening. It was the worst mob I've ever seen at Ninian. Hats off to them."

West Ham's ICF

When West Hams Inter City Firm burst onto our screens in the 80's in the 'Hooligan Documentary' with their massive mob and their Stanley knives, everyone suddenly realised how mental they were and meeting them was a brown underpants experience for many firms. (See Kersy's trip there in '79) They've never actually done much in Cardiff due perhaps to massive amounts of police when they come. They did once try to invade the Bob Bank at Cardiff but were repelled. If they had got on there, it would have been bloodshed like when Chelsea did and took a terrible beating despite putting up a top fight. Groups of Cardiff have bumped into the ICF all over the country and some terrible battles have occurred. Like the time described in the 'Soul Crew' where Dave Jones recalls the time their train pulled into a station and hundreds of West Ham piled on, battering everyone in sight. He says, "We were treated to the sight of West Ham taking it in turns to stamp on some poor fucker's head." The ghost of previous beatings was exorcised a few years back however when Cardiff ran the ICF down the Barking Road and basically showed them who's the Daddy.

Middlesbrough's Frontline

Many hooligan books have described a trip to Boro as a nightmare. They used to have massive numbers in the 80's, loads of big massive bastards and were game as fuck. A coach of us nearly found this out back in the mid 80's when, after having a game at Darlington abandoned, we attempted to get to a Boro v West Ham game, except the police wouldn't let us and turned us back. They probably did us a right favour. Another time in London, six of us were surrounded by about 30 Boro, massive horrible bastards who thought we were ICF. Luckily for us, they let us go, for which they get my total respect as they would have murdered us.

They came down to Cardiff once and plotted up in the Albert, sat quietly and waited for Cardiff to come. When a small group of Cardiff lads approached them they piled out, all horrible big grizzlies, throwing glasses and had Cardiff straight on their toes. If Cardiff had been more organised, weight of numbers would have overwhelmed the Boro but as usual, Cardiff's lack of organisation meant mobs spread out everywhere and another firm gets away with taking the piss through their ability to organise themselves. This is Cardiff's downfall. Often we will take thousands to a game, be split up all over the place and when it kicks off, we are all over the place. The only time Cardiff can ever say they were properly organised was in the early Soul Crew days with Annis at the helm from, I would say, about 83 until 86 when it all went to shit after raids, arrests etc. Since then, although they have a hell of a lot of lads, Cardiff are a disorganised rabble. I can testify to that after having a few kickings over the years which did not need to happen. If only we had been together and not split up all over the place.

Southampton

Now I've never rated Southampton. Been there loads of times and apart from minor scuffles, seen nothing of a mob. I know they bricked our coaches once but apart from that, a trip there is classed as a piss-up day only and no-one ever worries about walking freely around there. I find this surprising as usually seaside places are rough as fuck. Don't know what went wrong there. Anyway, first game of this season (2008) about 25 Southampton lads came to Cardiff and walked around to one of Cardiff's pubs, The Cornwall and banged on the windows calling Cardiff out. A group of lads came out and a toe-to-toe scrap went off in which although Southampton deserve respect for going there and having a go, they were absolutely slaughtered with two of their lads ending up in hospital for stitches. Fair play to them for going there. They had no idea what was in the pub and it must have taken some serious bottle. Ten out of ten for effort.

Sheffield Utd

In 1982, Sheffield brought 20-30 who attacked a Cardiff pub with 100 odd lads in it. Needless to say they took a fair old beating but respect goes to them for trying. In the early naughties, Cardiff went to Bramall Lane. Some of the lads that went said it was mayhem and Sheffield had hundreds of lads although a lot were chavs. After a lot of goading on the internet, Cardiff only took bout 50 lads but also a lot of game shirters. The Chief of Police in Sheffield said, "The level of violence shown towards my officers from the Welsh following was very high." I spoke to a Sheffield Utd fan who told me that last time he came to Cardiff, he was slyly jumped from behind and ended up in Cardiff Infirmary with a fractured cheekbone after youngsters took turns to score a goal with his head. He told me that when teams go to Sheffield, all the scum off the local estates come out, tooled up and attack the away fans regardless of whether they are scarfers or not. This was proved last week when Cardiff played at Bramall Lane. A mob of Sheffield attacked the buses and smashed some windows, injuring kids. A load of Cardiff's 'beer monsters' (not hooligans, just big fellas who like a beer but will fight if attacked) jumped off the coach and a furious battle went off toe-to-toe for a good three minutes until Sheffield realised they were getting damaged and ran. See pictures in here of kids injured by the brick throwing wankers. Also scuffles occurred outside the ground.

Here's Wayne's version of events.

"Fighting yesterday up Sheffield. I came out of away end. I was pissed and about 15 Sheffield ran at us. I just stood there. They went back. About 10 of us thought 'fuck it' so I sprinted after them and then realised that I was way out in front. Outside their pub up the top of the hill, I smashed into one, then had some good smacks! They were smashed and then the horses rushed in. Fights kicking off everywhere with Old Bill. It was a top day."

Swindon

These guys haven't got much of a mob. They had maybe 50-100 in the 80's. We had some drama with them back then when, after they kicked a Plymouth scarfer to death, a small group of us went up there when they were at home to Bradford. (See 'Soul Crew Seasiders' published by www.lulu.com) Lately when Cardiff have gone there though, it's been a walkover. The South Wales Echo ran a story a few years back which said that about ten Swindon fans had run through a family's house while they were watching TV, saying, "Sorry, we're being chased by Cardiff fans." When Cardiff went there in a pre-season friendly this season, some Taffies went to their pub and offered them out. A few slaps were given and Swindon shit themselves. End of. They have a few lads but they are small time compared to Cardiff.

Birmingham's Zulus

One of the most dangerous mobs around at home in the 80's. Always carrying blades and hanging round New Street station waiting for the unsuspecting. In 2006 a coach of them travelled down to South Wales and parked up on Barry Island about ten miles from Cardiff. They then sneaked into Cardiff in taxis. Cardiff had a horrible mob in the pubs waiting for them (see photos) but by the time they turned up at the Kings Pub in Canton, kick-off had started and most of the locals had gone to the match. It went off with a few stragglers that were there but was quickly over as the police arrived. Had they come half an hour earlier, there would have been a bloodbath for sure as this is regarded by some as Cardiff's HQ. In the ground they played up, throwing seats and coins and three stewards were injured in scuffles, one losing an eye. Playing up in the ground like this is madness as six of them found out four months later when their doors were kicked in one morning and they were arrested for Violent Disorder. They did look a good firm in the ground mind.

Shrewsbury's EBF (English Border Front)

These guys have had many clashes with the Welsh over the years. Wrexham have had many a battle with them and it was reported that a Wrexham stag night went there and running battles kicked off all night. Cardiff fans have also had a few run ins here. I was there when Cardiff absolutely wrecked and looted the town, turning cars and police vehicles upside down and causing thousands of pounds worth of damage. I ended up getting a kicking there after a small group of us became isolated. See the Urban Guerrillas section of this book for more stories about the EBF. The EBF turned up once in Swansea, 30 handed and wandered around the town dropping calling cards and thinking this was another silly Welsh Hick town. Eventually they bumped into 200 Jacks who absolutely slaughtered them. They totally underestimated Swansea who can raise some serious thugs when at home. It is said that an ancient bye-law still exists in Shrewsbury which allows for the shooting of a Welshman by crossbow after 6:00pm. This may explain the hatred.

Stockport

A week after they ran riot at small time Caernarvon, letting off smoke bombs and slapping scarfers, we played them up there. They found that an actual mob is not so easy to terrorise and even though we were massively outnumbered, we took it to them all round the town. It had kicked off all day and at the end of it we walked back to the station with a police escort and they lined the road clapping us in respect. We've met them a few times since and they have some tidy lads but they are no match for Cardiff. Simple as that. Respect to them for that day in the 80's though. They had about 200 good lads and were well up for it.

Walsall v Wrexham 2004
Walsall fans caused havoc in Wrexham town centre, burned a Welsh flag and hurled 'racist abuse' at police officers according to the newspapers. They said the Walsall mob then wrecked the train back to the Midlands and dogs were needed to prevent them getting off at Shrewsbury. According to the newspapers, they had an eight month pregnant woman in tears on the train as well, the brave twats. Typical of the new breed of hooligan these days, a lot of them are just chavs and don't know the meaning of the word respect. You imagine the chavs in your area, only they have a massive football crowd to hide in to cause anti-social nuisance? That's these guys.

West Brom
West Brom came to Cardiff about 50 handed and were nearly murdered. All their coach windows were put through. Up there, they did the same attacking the Valley Rams coaches, putting windows through and attacking the Cardiff fans. Several West Brom fans received long jail sentences for this attack.

Sheffield Wednesday v Cardiff 2008
A coach full of Cardiff travelled up there after a night in a club and by the time they arrived, they were a little the worse for wear. With no Sheffield mob about, bad behaviour in a pub ended up with scuffles with the police and a load of arrests for public order offences. One famous character was at his first game after coming off a ban and ended up with another ban and a session at Alcoholics Anonymous for his trouble. The Cardiff lads had a top day up there although most of them can't remember fuck all about it.

Pompey 657
These guys gave us the run-around a few times in the 80's and when I went down there in the early 90's, it was one of the best nights of my life. Fights were going off everywhere. However, at the FA Cup final this year they showed that their mob days are over and all they can do these days is bully and attack small groups. Shame as they were up there with the best back in the day.

Plymouth The Central Element

These guys have had a good little mob over the years at home and there have been several clashes between them and Cardiff, most notably the Britannia pub incident. (See 'Soul Crew' by Rivers and Jones) Seemingly finished now, like many others, but they have my respect for clashes I've had with them at football and in Butlins etc.

Wolves

Another well dangerous place to go back in the 80's. You were always guaranteed a scrap at Wolves and according to one of their books, they had a 'bag man' who would walk around with holdall full of blades ready for when it kicked off. Horrible bastards. Trips to Wolves these days are usually bubble trips and West Midlands police are well known bastards who will nick you for anything. They recently brought a good firm to Cardiff and kicked off a bit in the ground but never met our mob properly due to massive police overkill.

Fulham

In '93, a small group of Cardiff invaded the Fulham end and clashed with them although their numbers were swelled by Chelsea. Loads more Cardiff jumped the fence and piled in giving the Cockneys a good slapping. Cardiff lads said Fulham had a good go and deserve a bit of respect for their efforts.

Stoke the Naughty Forty

When we went there in 2000, it was absolute chaos. Every Cardiff lad who was anyone was there and after the game it was mental. The footage speaks for itself and Cardiff's mob that day was mental. After the police had taken their kicking off the Taffies, they were then subjected to a whole night of violence and terror from Stoke's mob which also numbered many hundreds. Over the years, we've had a lot of run-ins with Stoke at football and away and I respect them as one of the best. I remember when two of them jumped onto the pitch at Ninian and ran at Nathan Blake who shit his pants. Funny that as Blakey's supposed to be a bit of a brawler but he was grizzling to the Echo about how "he would have had a go but they could have had knives." Yeh, ok bruv. They were going to stab you on national TV were they? Ya big baby.

Over Butlins, I had a few incidents of fisticuffs with Stoke lads and I have spoken to them about the incidents at Britannia and they admitted that if Cardiff had got through the last fence, they think they would have been fucked. We had the numbers and the quality lads. Many firms would never admit something like that, so respect all round there for Stoke.

Chapter Fifteen
The Future

So what does the future hold for the mobs of Wales? It looks bleak for them to be honest. CCTV, banning orders, harsh prison sentences and harassment of known hooligans are all taking their toll on the numbers prepared to get involved. Welsh fans travelling away are often subjected to 'bubble matches' where coaches have to meet at a prearranged rendezvous point to exchange tokens for match tickets. They are then ferried straight in and out of towns, not allowed anywhere near a pub or to drink on the coach. At Paddington when Cardiff were away to Millwall, large scale searching of fans led to dozens of arrests for weapons and drugs and the Millwall coach was also searched en route to Swansea and found to be crammed with weapons.

Drug dogs are also being used in the grounds. In 2007 at Swansea's home game against Brighton, 22 fans were given warnings as police used sophisticated equipment to check fans for the presence of cocaine and cannabis. No drugs were found on these people but you can bet their names were given to the drug squad for future use. Another tool increasingly being used is 'Association' where the police film people with no criminal record mixing with known hooligans in pubs, etc and then ban them from the ground. Guilt by association. When it comes to football, your 'human rights' go out the window.

Such has been the effect on Cardiff's Soul Crew's numbers that as described earlier, at a home match against bitter enemies Newport, the hooligan element could only manage to get 40 together to try and have a go at the visitors. Not so long ago, there would have been hundreds of thugs out for such a game. This was severely embarrassing for Cardiff's hooligan element but many of the main faces simply don't bother anymore as it's not worth the hassle for them as much as it hurts them to let strangers wander about giving it large.

The Story of the Park 20, by Jay
"Word was put out weeks before that Newport were bringing a massive mob to Ninian and that they wanted it big time. They haven't had a big tear up at Cardiff since the 80's and they wanted revenge for the savage kicking their 15 lads received in Milan. We had told EVERYONE to meet up in Grangetown but when we

arrived, there was only a pathetic little bunch. Whilst we are in the pub, some Under 5's come running in to announce that Newport's escort was by the Black and White Café and were fighting the Old Bill trying to get away. We ran down to the park to confront them. On the way, we met some geezer on a bike who said, "There's 400 of them boys, you gonna have them?" We said, "Oh yeh, all 20 of us" and he rode off on his bike saying he was off to suss things out. It was like a comedy sketch. We ran into the park and this is a rag tag bunch now comprising four or five fatties, a team of teenagers, Lenny Lip, a guy with a wooden leg and two 14 year olds. As the 400 strong mob saw us, they all started shouting and some tried to break the escort. Clanger said to the guy with the wooden leg, "If it goes off, I'm having that leg as a tool." It was well hilarious.

The Old Bill charged into the park and let the dogs go, so on our toes we went. As we ran from the dogs, one of the kids' carrier bags split and cans of 'Orangeeboom' went flying everywhere. They couldn't stop to pick them up as snarling mutts were running towards us looking to rip arse. A friend who's a steward in the ground said it came over the radio that the police were panicking as they thought it was a large mob of Cardiff coming out of the darkness to attack the escort. When they realised that it was only 20, the panic was over. We joke that they were about to send a van to nick us, then decided to send the Sunshine Variety Club coach instead. At least we showed up and they faced some resistance. We later had a go at another escort, this time with 40 but compared to the old days of the Soul Crew, this is shit and it proved the Old Bill have smashed the Soul Crew."

At the time of writing, Cardiff have drawn Swansea away. This would have been a dream trip for the hooligans of South Wales in the past and would have brought out all the old faces, people who hadn't been to football for ages plus hordes of thugs who never go to football would have been out on the streets in the hopes of a scrap. However, it's not worth anyone getting excited about as Cardiff fans are only allowed 1500 tickets. All away fans will have to go on special buses arranged by the police and meet them at the services just outside Swansea to exchange vouchers for match tickets before being bussed straight to the ground and then straight back out again after the game.

No-one will be allowed to travel by train and the police have said anyone arriving in Swansea without tickets will be arrested. There will be massive amounts of police with helicopters and allsorts. The whole thing from a hooligan point of view, will be a waste of time.

Chav Street Hooligans

Cardiff, as well as a lot of other teams, seem to attract massive numbers of chavvy little cunts who've seen 'Green Street' and think they can use the cover of being in a large group to make nuisances of themselves. This problem came to a head at Cardiff recently where one group of chavs had to be 'spoken to' by the old school lads for their general anti-social behaviour and threats to other young Cardiff fans. It soon stopped!

Will it ever end?

Mind you, even with all these heavy duty sentences and clampdowns and raids, police harassment in pubs and workplaces, hooliganism still plods along. This season already there has been trouble at pre-season friendlies in Swindon, Merthyr, fighting with Sunderland and Celtic in Portugal and trouble with Southampton and Sheffield United. So it looks as if this phenomenon will plod along forever. Despite all the arrests, CCTV, harassment etc, the trouble goes on.

Will it ever end?

Thanks to all the people
who have helped me put this book together.

Too many to name all of you
but you know who you are.

www.hooligancentral.co.uk